# COLLIER OF MANCHESTER

## A FRIEND'S TRIBUTE

BY

### GEORGE JACKSON

HODDER AND STOUGHTON
LIMITED          LONDON

| | | | |
|---|---|---|---|
| *First Edition* | . . . | *Printed October* | *1923* |
| *Second Edition* | . . | *Printed November 1923* | |
| *Third Edition* | . . . | *Printed December 1923* | |

Made and Printed in Great Britain.
T. and A. CONSTABLE LTD., Printers, Edinburgh.

# PREFACE

THIS is not a formal biography ; it is rather, as the title-page indicates, the tribute of a friend. In Collier's case, the materials for a volume of the familiar ' Life and Letters ' order do not exist. Very few of his letters have been preserved. Except for a few months of his first year after leaving college he kept no diary. Only five of his sermon manuscripts remain, and these are all earlier than his Manchester days. He wrote no books, and only very occasionally a brief magazine article. Journalists who interviewed him found him always ready to talk about his work, always reluctant to talk about himself. With one or two exceptions, even his most intimate friends have been able to contribute very few characteristic and self-revealing sayings or incidents. As one of them says, Collier was ' more given to laughter than epigrams.' If, therefore, the reader sometimes finds the following pages lacking in concrete and picturesque detail, if he has to listen to Collier speaking through me, when he would rather have heard him speaking for himself, he has the explanation in advance. Such material as I have been able to gather has been obtained mainly from correspondence and interviews with old colleagues, friends, and fellow-workers, from newspaper cuttings, and from old volumes of the monthly magazine and the annual reports of the Manchester Mission. Again and again the weary search of hours in what is now only a heap of dead and dry chaff has been rewarded with but the tiniest handful of grains of wheat. At the same time, this record, brief as it is, will, I think, be found trustworthy. Nothing has been set down for which there was not written or oral testimony ; and as these pages have been carefully read both by Mrs. Collier, her son (the Rev. Donald Collier, B.A.), and by Collier's successor—the Rev. Herbert Cooper—the substantial accuracy of the narrative may be safely assumed. Of course, this does not involve them or anyone else in any responsibility for the estimate of Collier's life and work which is here given. For that the writer himself is alone responsible.

Two further words may be added : one about the man, the other about his work. More than two years have passed since Collier's death, but there is no sign of weakness or decay in the work to which he gave his life. His sudden removal left many fearing for the stability of the Manchester Mission ; but what, under other circumstances, might have proved a disastrous shock has only revealed the depth and strength of the foundations which he had laid.  He had piled high, but he had dug deep, and therefore his work abides.  Of the man himself I have only to say that, having known him with some intimacy for thirty years, my affection and regard have steadily increased with the nearer view of him which the writing of this book has given me.

I am greatly indebted to scores of correspondents and friends without whose aid these pages could never have been written.  It is impossible to name them all here, but besides Mrs. Collier and Mr. Cooper, a word of special acknowledgment is due to the Rev. Samuel Marriott and to Gipsy Smith for the very helpful memoranda with which they have furnished me.  The index is the work of my wife, who has also been my counsellor and helper throughout.

GEORGE JACKSON.

Didsbury College,
*July* 1923.

# CONTENTS

# CHAPTER I

## EARLY YEARS

### 1855–1881

Not long ago a man out of work found his way to the Men's Home of the Manchester Mission. It was by no means his first visit, but several years had passed since he had been there last. During the interval S. F. Collier, the founder of the Home, had died. As the man stood waiting in the office, he caught sight of a portrait of Collier which hung on the wall. Pulling himself up sharply before the picture he stood for a few seconds at attention. Then he said, half to himself but loud enough to be overheard by one who was standing by, ' You 're the man that was always sorry for coves like I.' This is the man whose story the following pages seek to tell—a man who for nearly forty years bore on his mind and heart the sins and sorrows of the great city in which he lived ; who daily remembered and was ' sorry for ' the dim multitudes whom most of us find it so easy to forget, except perhaps at Christmas, or when some grave industrial crisis thrusts hunger's gaunt visage before our eyes, and who never wearied devising new ways of helping them ; a man to whom it was given, as to very few of his generation, to build up good and honest citizens out of the mere driftwood of the great human tide, and who, when he died, left his best and most abiding memorial in the lives of the thousands whose weary lot he had lightened, and whose feet he had brought up out of the miry clay.

SAMUEL FRANCIS COLLIER was born in Runcorn, Cheshire, on October 3, 1855. His mother, Mary Littler, was the second wife of Samuel Collier, and Samuel Francis was their eldest son. Of Mrs. Collier, unfortunately, there is little to be told. Her son once said of her that ' she was always calm when there was bustle everywhere else,' and at the time of his death she was spoken of as ' a quiet, godly woman of rare charm and simplicity of manner ' ; but beyond this no record survives. The father appears to have been a man of unusual strength of character and of considerable local fame. He was one of a large family all of whom were deeply religious, well versed in the Scriptures, and keenly interested in the problems of theology. They studied and discussed together books like Watson's *Institutes*, and of one of them it is related that he liked nothing better than to join in public debate, say, with the local Baptist minister on the subject of infant baptism. In all this warm, quick life Samuel Collier shared to the full. His business life began at Preston Brook, a few miles from Runcorn, and here his first married days were spent. Later he removed to Runcorn, where he established a large and successful grocery business.

It says much both for his own will to get on and for the harder conditions of life seventy years ago, that in order to meet the requirements of customers who had to go early to work, his shop used to be open every morning at five o'clock. Nor were the claims of the larger life of the town forgotten. He was one of the ' Improvement Commissioners ' for Runcorn—the Town Council of those days—and whenever a fight was on, Samuel Collier was usually to be found in the thick of it. But through all, the Church remained his first and strongest love. In his early days he was a member of the Primitive Methodist Church, and it was there that he began his long and remarkable career as a lay preacher. Indeed, there is good reason to believe that at one time he contemplated going farther and seeking admission into its ministry, but an early marriage and other circumstances which are now obscure put an end to that project and at the same time led him to become a Wesleyan Methodist.

Samuel Collier was one of that great band of lay preachers to whom Methodism in all its branches owes so incalculable a debt. If one may judge by the few letters to his son which have been preserved, he thought a good deal more about sermons and preachers than about either his shop or his municipal politics.[1] His fame as an evangelist went abroad through all Cheshire. An old lady

[1] Generally, of course, it is of preachers of his own Church that he writes ; but on one occasion—September 1875—he tells of going to hear Cardinal Manning in Liverpool : ' He is a clever speaker and can reason well,' is the rather disappointingly meagre verdict.

who heard the son preach while he was a student at Didsbury remarked afterwards, ' He will make his mark, but he can't yet preach like his father.' Very sure of his message, fearless, passionate, often vehement, in the proclamation of it, his word sometimes shook men's very souls.   He was a tall man, with dark, flashing eyes, and abundant gesture, and when he preached he put all his powers to work. If his preaching had little of the ' wooing note ' in it, it sometimes crashed through the door of men's hearts by the sheer energy of conviction which lay behind it.   When he was in the pulpit, it used to be said, sinners either ' came out ' or ' went out ' ; that is to say, they either went forward to the ' penitent form,' or fled from the presence of a preacher who reasoned with such power of righteousness and judgment.   For his own as well as for his son's sake, we should have been glad to know more of this remarkable man.   He was a man universally esteemed for his strict uprightness and loyalty to conviction ;  but he had, apparently, none of the warmth and geniality of his son.   There was about him a certain stern reserve which made him more feared than loved.   As Matthew Arnold said of Gray, he never spoke out—unless it was in the pulpit ;  even his letters to his son seem, when all allowance is made, rather cold and formal. When Francis writes from school to ask his father's guidance in the choice of a profession, he gets little more than this :  ' It is well to have the counsel and advice of parents and friends, but it is better

to have the light and teaching which is from above.'
When the boy preached for the first time in St.
Paul's Church, Runcorn—the church in which he
had worshipped as a child—and all others were
speaking words of commendation and encourage-
ment, the father's only comment was that he would
have to do much better than that to satisfy him.
Nevertheless, one is glad to think that the old man
lived long enough to be warmed and gladdened by
the promise of his son's early ministry in the south
of England. He died in October 1883, just two
years before Samuel Francis began his great work
in Manchester.

We get a few, a very few, glimpses of young
Collier in these early Runcorn days. The life of
the home, as of most Methodist homes sixty or
seventy years ago, was simple, perhaps even austere,
but there does not seem to have been about it anything forced or unnatural. Nobody who knew
S. F. Collier in later life will believe that he and
merry laughter were ever far apart. Prompted
partly perhaps by his father's vigorous performances
in the pulpit, ' Master Frank ' acquired considerable
reputation as a reciter, and was much in demand
at children's parties. He had his full share of the
mishaps which usually fall to the lot of healthy
boys with anything of the spirit of adventure in
them. On one occasion an involuntary dip in the
Bridgewater Canal nearly cost him his life. At
another time a bit of old wire pierced one of his
eyes, with results which for a while threatened to

be very grave ; permanent injury to the sight was happily averted, but the mark of the mishap was with him to the end.   Perhaps the most character-istic of these memories of childhood is a story which, in varying versions, was often repeated in later days at Collier's expense.   He had been sent on an errand with a couple of parcels.   Shortly after-wards he was discovered with a boy on each side of him, each carrying a parcel, while S. F. C. marched between them unburdened and free.   His friends liked to recall the little parable in after years when they saw his astonishing knack of setting others to work, though they knew well that it told only half the truth : whatever burdens Collier laid upon others the heaviest end was always kept for himself.

School-days began at Mill House Academy, Run-corn, kept by a Mr. Bower ; but a new and im-portant chapter in the boy's life opened in 1868 when, at the age of thirteen, he went to Bickerton House, Southport.   Here he spent the next nine years—six as pupil and three as tutor.   The head of the school was the late Henry Mathwin, a man of fine intellectual gifts and of still rarer moral qualities.   The teacher's opportunity was in his eyes a sacred trust from on high, and he did his work always as one who must give an account. When he died—in January 1908—Collier, who gave an address at the grave-side, spoke not only for himself but for hundreds of old Bickerton House boys when he said that next to his own father he

owed more to Mr. Mathwin and to his teaching than
to any one else in the world. The Rev. G. Armstrong Bennetts, who joined the staff of the school
while Collier was still one of its pupils, writes as
follows of the influence of its head master :—

> ' I never knew any school in which there was
> so fine a tone of moral and religious life. Mr.
> Mathwin was an intense admirer of Arnold of
> Rugby, and modelled his school management
> much upon the lines adopted by Arnold. He
> drew his elder boys into close and affectionate
> comradeship with himself, and urged his assistant
> masters to carry the same tone through the
> school. He would not allow any system of
> punishments in the discipline of the school. He
> had himself a genius for managing boys and he
> expected his masters to rule by the exercise of
> gentle but firm personal influence. I never
> knew anywhere a more beautiful tone of com-
> radeship than existed in Bickerton House, which
> won high distinction not only in its scholastic
> results but in character-building.'

In this kindly, fostering air Collier made steady
if not brilliant progress with his studies. He passed
the Cambridge Local Examinations, Junior and
Senior, both with honours, obtaining in the latter
distinction in French. A year or two later he took
the London Matriculation, again with honours.
Nor were his successes confined to the class-room.
Old ' Bickertonians ' still remember and talk of
his prowess on the cricket-field, especially with
the ball. Indeed, for two or three years he
was the team's ' crack ' bowler. His analysis as

recorded in the *Bickerton Annual* for 1876 read as
follows :—

| Balls. | Runs. | Maidens. | Wickets. | Wides. | No-Balls. | Runs per Wicket. |
|---|---|---|---|---|---|---|
| 668 | 182 | 42 | 60 | 2 | 6 | 3·16 |

And, as we shall see, Collier's interest in the national
game never slackened to the end of his life.   Meanwhile, more serious matters were beginning to
occupy his mind.   Bickerton House was a Methodist school, and on Sundays the boys attended the
Trinity Wesleyan Methodist Church in Southport.
One of the class-leaders connected with the Church
was Mr. Thomas Walton Stead, of whose class
several of the assistant masters and some of the
senior boys, including Collier, were members.   Mr.
Armstrong Bennetts, who was also a member of
the class at this time, describes its leader as ' a
man of most refined and gentle personality, a man
of culture and of deep and fervent piety.'   So that
once again young Collier was supremely fortunate
in the character of the personal influences that
were helping to mould his life during its most
plastic years.   It was at one of the meetings of
Mr. Stead's class, greatly aided by his tutor,
Mr. Bennetts—whose service at this crisis of his
life he always gratefully acknowledged—that Collier,
then a boy of sixteen, made the religious decision
which was to determine all his own future.[1]   There

[1] Another member of Mr. Walton Stead's class who left a very deep
impression on Collier's mind was a simple, unlettered, but godly old
man, known among his fellow-members as ' blind William '—an interesting illustration of that spiritual *camaraderie* which the Methodist
class-meeting makes possible, and ought to cultivate, among Christian men
and women of the most diverse types.

are two or three references to what had taken place in his letters to his parents, but on the whole it seems better not to quote them. They are very brief, they are mixed up in schoolboy fashion with other interests of his daily life, and they are couched, naturally enough, in the conventional religious phraseology of the day. The real significance of the change is to be looked for, not in his own boyish account of it, but in the ' clear life ensuing.'

True to his lifelong instinct, Collier had no sooner ' enlisted ' himself than he set about seeking recruits. He undertook the distributing of tracts in the neighbourhood of his school, and during one of his holidays his new faith for the first time found public speech for itself in a little cottage meeting held in what is still known in Runcorn as ' Taylor's Row.' To that humble beginning he used always to trace his first impulse to do the work of an evangelist. A year or two later he preached his first sermon as a local preacher. His text was Luke xviii. 37 : ' They told him that Jesus of Nazareth passeth by.' He evidently took great pains with this first effort. Three copies of the manuscript are still in existence, one of which bears a pencilled note which suggests that it had been submitted to a friend for criticism and counsel. It is dated February 26, 1874. Another copy is inscribed, in the handwriting of a later day, ' S. F. C.'s first sermon, preached at Birkdale Common, Southport.' The following year, according to Methodist usage, he had to preach his

' trial sermon ' before receiving his full credentials
as a lay preacher. ' I am afraid,' his father writes
to him, ' you think too much about it. My advice
is, prepare as if you were going to address a congregation in the usual way. Try to be yourself,
preach as one intent on doing good, and all will be
right.' The ordeal was successfully passed, and at
twenty years of age Collier found himself enrolled
among the fully accredited lay preachers of the
Wesleyan Methodist Church.

And now the time was approaching when a
definite decision must be taken about the future
course of his life. In a letter to his parents, March 6,
1872, he had said, referring to possible further
examinations, ' I should like to know what I am
going to take as a profession, but I cannot decide.'
Successful though he was as a teacher, he does not
seem ever to have contemplated devoting himself
to the calling of a schoolmaster. Probably his
strongest ambition in these early years was to
become a barrister. During his holidays, it is said,[1]
he used to spend much of his time in the Law Courts
of Liverpool, listening to the speeches of contending
counsel. And there is, perhaps, a further indica-
tion of this leaning in the fact that the only allusion,
in the small batch of his home letters which have
been preserved, to any events outside the world of
home, school, and Church, is to the famous Tich-
borne trial. But his conversion, the influence of
his father's example, and his own keen interest in

[1] Obituary notice, *Minutes of Conference,* 1921.

all the activities of his Church, together with the judgment of others who watched his steadily developing powers, all combined to draw him another way, and in the spring of 1877 he offered himself as a candidate for the Wesleyan Methodist ministry. The only reference that I have been able to discover to his experiences under the manifold tests to which all such candidates must submit themselves is in a speech delivered by himself during his year of office as President of the Conference. Speaking at a crowded meeting in the old Standishgate Church, Wigan, he said, ' This is not the first time I have spoken in this place. I preached one of my trial sermons here, and I had then an audience of nine. They tried to sing the first hymn three times, and broke down each time. The superintendent minister reported that the young man preached fairly well, but lacked fire ! That report,' Collier added, ' nearly damned my reputation as an evangelist.' However, he got through, and the next autumn he was sent to Didsbury College, Manchester, to begin his training for the work of his life.

During the summer of the same year Collier received the following letter from his old head master :—

' MY DEAR COLLIER,—Now that all is clear, so far as I can see, for your going to Didsbury, I must send a line to congratulate you and say how pleased I am that your footsteps have been directed thitherward. I think I can see the

hand of the Lord in this; doubtless you ca*
also. Years ago I thought your providentia
path lay in the direction you have chosen, anc
you will scarcely believe it, or at any rate are
scarcely prepared to hear me say how much m*
heart ached if I saw the slightest divergence
as I fancied, from that path. I prayed that
your Heavenly Father would guide you, and *
prayed too that I might have grace and wisdon
vouchsafed to say a word to help to form you*
character for this important, awfully important
work of the ministry.

'From time to time I hope to see you to hea*
how you are getting on, when I shall probabl*
take the opportunity and the liberty of advising.
praising, or blaming, as the case may be. I*
the latter, you know what wonderful energy *
can throw into a scolding. So, beware, youn*
man! If I have reason to think you are no*
studying according to a *system*, if I find you hav*
not a well-ordered routine to which you ar*
closely sticking, if I have reason to think yo*
are not setting your face like a rock against al*
the enticements of your good-natured friends t*
take you from that routine, then, *then*, THEN.
unhappy youth! a storm rising in Bickerton
House will crash about your poor devoted head.
*Comprenez-vous ?*

'I must take this opportunity of thanking
you for all the good you have done among my
boys. God has blessed your care and anxiety
to their good. All the boys, young and old,
and not only the boys but the masters and
household, regret your leaving. To continue
the good you have done you cannot do better
than write occasionally to —— and ——.[1] I
shall be glad to know you are doing this.

[1] Presumably boys who had been specially committed to Collier's care.

'And now I have only to say that any time you will be very welcome at my house and among my family. In the kind note I got from you you said Bickerton House had been to you as a home; please consider it still as such. Visit us when you have opportunity and you will soon find that the house is still open to you.

'God bless and guide you!—Yours affectionately, H. MATHWIN.'

The letter is interesting alike as a revelation of the kindly heart of the worthy schoolmaster and of the place which Collier had won for himself in the life of the school. The words about his personal influence with the boys were no idle compliment. Mr. Mathwin's daughter-in-law tells me that it was no uncommon thing for unusually difficult cases to be put under his special care : she remembers one instance in which a boy's movements from class to class were determined entirely by Collier's, in order that the two might not be separated. It is pleasant, too, to know that the happy personal relations which the letter indicates were maintained to the last. At Mr. Mathwin's death, as we have already seen, and again at his son's and grandson's—a victim of the Great War—it fell to Collier to pay the last tribute of affection and esteem. Not less enduring were the ties which bound him to his old school-fellows. ' One vivid memory,' a colleague of later years writes, ' is of my dropping in on him on the eve of a Mission Anniversary to find him busily conning a small memorandum book of subscribers. In reply to my inquiry as to how things were going he told me, tapping the book as he did so, that no less than thirteen hundred pounds out of the three thousand odd that he was asking for that year had come, or was coming, out of the pockets of the old boys of Bickerton House, Southport, his own old school of which he always spoke with great affection.'

The usual period of college residence for a student preparing for the ministry of the Wesleyan Method-ist Church is three years,[1] followed by four on pro-bation. In Collier's case the college term was extended by a year in consequence of a break-down in his health, so that Didsbury continued to be his home from 1877 to 1881—four of the forty years which in all he was destined to spend within the Manchester area. On the staff of the college at that time were Dr. J. Dury Geden, a member of the Old Testament Revision Company, and Dr. W. Burt Pope, 'theologian, mystic, saint,' as he is rightly named in the tablet to his memory in the college chapel. But nothing remains to indicate the nature or extent of the young student's debt to these devout and learned teachers. Perhaps, as not infrequently happens, he gained more from the friendly clash of mind with mind in the frank and free fellowship of college life than in the more formal instruction of the class-room. His relations with

[1] In comparing this with, say, the seven years of a Scottish Presby-terian student's life, account must be taken both of the greater length of the college year—from the beginning of September to the middle of June—and of the four probationary years that follow.

is fellow-students were of the happiest kind. In he limp Didsbury air, as J. M. Barrie said of old John Stuart Blackie, Collier carried his breeze with him. Who could withstand the infection of that light-hearted laugh ? On the cricket field he repeated his Bickerton House exploits, so that when he was President old Didsbury associates would often introduce him as the man who used to bowl them out. He had, too, as many a fellow-worker learned in after years, the gift of talking plainly to a man for his good without forfeiting his goodwill. ' I was very young when I went to Didsbury,' writes a fellow-student who has since risen to high Connexional office, ' and he was a third year man when I entered. As a Southerner, I suppose I was a little bit shy and somewhat reserved, and this was mistaken by some of my friends ; for one day Collier called me into his " den," gave me a tremendous rating for putting on so much " side," and told me I was making myself somewhat disliked by the men generally. It came as a surprise, but it was a wholesome corrective.'

As a student, while his scholastic record was in no way remarkable, Collier continued the good work he had begun at Bickerton House and kept his place among the best men of the college. In 1878 he passed the ' Inter Arts ' examination of the London University, and secured the first prize offered to the men of his year. At that time, apparently, mathematics was his favourite study ; and, though one does not usually associate conic sections with the founder of the Manchester Mission, a younger contemporary well remembers being initiated by him into the mysteries of the ellipse and the parabola. He was also one of a small group of men who studied together Hebrew and the Greek Testament. They were S. F. Collier, F. L. Wiseman, F. J. Nance, V. W. Pearson, and G. J. Ayre. Three out of the five, it is worthy of note, have since been Presidents of the Conference —Collier and Wiseman in England, Nance in Australia. Indeed, the impression made on the mind of the younger contemporary already quoted was that of a student, quiet and restrained, logical and didactic, one more likely to develop into a college tutor than the head of a great city mission. But this is an impression of the Southport days. Possibly, too, if ever at that time Collier had allowed his own thoughts for the future to take shape, it is in some such form they would have floated before him. At any rate, there is his own authority for saying that when he entered college he had no consciousness of any *special* call to do the work of an evangelist. But he had not long been at Didsbury before it grew plain alike to himself and his fellows that God had other plans for him than the pursuits of the Christian scholar.

It is usual for men who are preparing for the Wesleyan Methodist ministry to spend their week ends conducting services in the churches of the towns and villages in the neighbourhood of the college which they attend. From the strictly academic point of view the custom is open to very obvious criticism, for it makes serious inroads upon the time available for classes and study; on the other hand, it has very real compensations for the students themselves, and it may be hoped also for the churches which they serve. A detailed register which Collier kept during his four years at Didsbury shows that altogether he conducted no fewer than from three to four hundred of these Sunday services. The register contains a list, not only of the places which he visited, and the homes in which he stayed, but also of the texts from which he preached, together with some brief general 'remarks.' The entries under both these latter heads show quite plainly the steady drift of his mind. The text from which he preached most frequently—students have not usually many sermons : we are all familiar with the ancient jests about the two dried tongues in the week-end bag— was Heb. vii. 25 : 'Able to save to the uttermost.' In the column for 'remarks' are jottings like these —interspersed, of course, with others in a more subdued key :—

'Preached in morning outside. School-room full in afternoon. Preached from 5 to 6 o'clock outside. Good congregation afterwards in chapel. About twelve found the Saviour.'

'Very good day. Addressed Sunday School in afternoon. Preached new sermon in the evening. Two or three decided.'

'Good times. H—— gave his heart to God ; so others.'

' Very poor congregation, or only moderate, in the morning. Very good in the evening. Enjoyed the day, and God was with us in manifested power.'

Old Didsbury men who recall their own experiences in the college chapel pulpit at the Thursday evening service will be interested in this : ' Very good time. Mr. Geden thanked me. *I felt God helped me. Remember this*, and never forget the help.' The following, too, deserves note as containing Collier's first mention of a man who was so powerfully to influence the whole of his own future life and work : ' Invited to open new mission room [at Oldham]. Place full both services. Many from Manchester Street. Rev. H. J. Pope present.' But perhaps the most significant of all these entries is the first. The day was spent at Lower and Higher Disley, in Cheshire : ' Enjoyed each service exceedingly. At evening service six penitents, five young men and a woman, found peace.'

It was this experience of his first Sunday at college—again there is Collier's own authority for the statement—which determined his career ; he had seen the heavenly vision, and he dare not disobey ; henceforth he knew himself set to do the work of an evangelist. Nor did he wait till college days were over in order to make a beginning. About a mile from Didsbury, in what was then the village of Heaton Mersey, was a small and struggling Methodist society. Hard by, scores of navvies were engaged in making a new railway from Stockport to Manchester. In this double fact Collier saw his opportunity. He brought the matter up at the college supper-table, and a plan of campaign was agreed upon. Collier himself, of course, was appointed commander-in-chief, and during a special three weeks' mission he daily led his fellow-students in squads to the village. He used every device that his inventive wit could suggest to attract the people and compel them to come in. He visited the ale-houses; he made friends with the navvies; he patrolled the village streets ringing the college dinner-bell; he held open-air meetings in all weathers; and, finally, by a bold and clever stroke of policy, he secured the good-will of a rather doubtful and reluctant vicar. All this meant inevitable and serious interference with the work of the class-room and the study. It is even said that in Collier's own case the authorities of the college consented for a time to release him from the usual obligations of a student's life. Certain it is that he never repeated the academic successes of his first year. But however much, on general grounds, we may doubt the wisdom of such a course, and however little we should be justified in arguing from an exceptional case like Collier's, no one will deny the value to him of this early evangelistic experiment. He missed his degree, but the navvies and ale-houses of Heaton Mersey taught him some things which he could never have learned from the lectures of William Burt

Pope or John Dury Geden. We may regret that a choice had to be made, for, like all students for the Christian ministry, he needed both; yet when we look back to-day and see how ' the Bishop of Heaton Mersey '—as he was often playfully called —was preparing the way for the future head of the Manchester Mission, it is perhaps best to be silent : ' There is a Hand that guides.' [1]

There is one question which may be asked before we leave Didsbury to follow Collier into the larger life of his public ministry. Did he pass through any sharp mental and spiritual crisis such as sometimes has made college days for ever unforgettable to a man ? One of his old Didsbury friends, in a letter to the *Methodist Recorder*, written just after Collier's death, says that ' he passed through a severe and prolonged spiritual crisis which searched his soul to the very depths.' What exactly lies behind this I do not know. No details are given, nor have I come upon any other allusions to such a conflict, either then or at any later time. A small book of manuscript prayers remains, dated 1881—the year he left Didsbury—but the entries are very few, and these mainly in preparation for the conduct of public worship. There are in them no marks of spiritual struggle, nor any intimate

---

[1] Another entry in the register of college appointments, dated Dec. 31, 1878, is : ' Heaton Mersey—Good time. Presented with Geikie's *Life of Christ.*' Thirty-five years later, by an interesting coincidence, his son, Donald, preached one of his trial sermons as a candidate for the ministry in the handsome church at Heaton Mersey which his father's successful labours had made both possible and necessary.

self-revelations of any kind whatever. The truth is, Collier was the least introspective of men. He saw religion almost wholly from the practical side. It was for him mainly a problem, not for thought, nor for thought and life, but simply for life. It is significant that when, many years after, a course of Sunday afternoon lectures was given in the Central Hall, Manchester, in defence of Christianity and in reply to Robert Blatchford, Collier chose as his own subject, ' The Miracle of Changed Lives.' Of course he believed in the miracles of the New Testament, and would have been ready to justify his faith ; but his chief interest was in the miracles, the moral miracles, of to-day. With all his heart he would have agreed with Dr. Denney when he says that the proof of the Gospel is ' dynamical, not logical. It is demonstrated, not by argument, but by what it does.' I am not, I hope, misjudging my friend in saying this ; it is the impression which he always left upon my mind, and I can recall nothing that he ever said or wrote which contradicts it.

# CHAPTER II

## TRYING HIS WINGS

### 1881–1885

COLLIER left Didsbury in the summer of 1881, and at the ensuing Conference received his first appointment. It proved to be of a wholly unexpected character : he was appointed ' District Missionary ' in Kent. For the sake of those who are unfamiliar with Methodist phraseology, it may be explained that British Wesleyan Methodism is divided, for the purposes of ecclesiastical administration, into thirty-five Districts. Years ago it was usual for Conference to appoint in many of these Districts a young, unmarried minister, of marked evangelistic gifts, to go to and fro within the District, conducting special services in the churches, both of town and country, with the purpose of quickening their spiritual life, and of bringing in the ' outsider.' Influenced, probably, by the report of what had taken place at Heaton Mersey, the Home Missionary Committee laid hands on Collier, and in September he found himself among the hop-fields and orchards of Kent with the commission of a roving evangelist. It was a task which appealed in many ways to his eager, adventurous spirit, and he threw himself into it with characteristic ardour. But it brought with it many drawbacks and not a few perils. During the greater part of the year he had no fixed abode. He moved from town to town, from village to village, never remaining in one place more than two or three weeks, and sometimes only for a few days. His mornings were given to visiting, his afternoons and evenings to public services, both outdoor and indoor. Under such circumstances, serious study was obviously impossible, and a glance at his sermon register is sufficient to show that the same little handful of addresses had to do duty again and again. His health suffered, and in every way the strain was greater than the inexperience and immaturity of youth ought to be called on to bear. It is doubtful, too, if there were compensating advantages to the churches which the missioner served. In many cases, without doubt, real and abiding good was done ; but too often the ' Special Mission ' meant only a brief spasm of unnatural activity which died down again into the old torpor as soon as the missioner had gone on his way. Collier himself felt very keenly the futility of much of this here-to-day-and-gone-to-morrow kind of evangelism, and on the whole we may be thankful that his perilous vagrancy came to an end with the end of the year. The Methodist Church, too, it may be added, has since grown wiser, and now no longer sends untried youth on quixotic adventures of this kind.

For the year, however, Collier did his duty manfully. There are, of course, few now who can recall those far-off days in Kent. Why should any one greatly concern himself with the doings of a young and unknown Methodist probationer? One vivid little memory, however, survives and may be here reproduced :—

'Dymchurch is a mere hamlet on the edge of Romney Marsh, five miles from Hythe and eight from Folkestone. A new chapel had just been built and opened, and Mr. Collier held a fortnight's Mission there in December 1881. He often spoke of the drive thither in an open trap, through a blinding snowstorm and a terrible east wind, expecting the trap to over-turn every minute. In those days the sea wall had not been built, and travellers along that road felt the full force of the wind from the sea. Those who have travelled along it even in summer, running as it does through a desolate, beach-covered country, flanked on its sea side by weird-looking Martello towers, can appreciate such a journey taken in the depth of winter, with the "sea-fret" covering the marsh, and the round towers, which at the time of the Napoleonic fright had been put along that low-lying coast to protect it, looming through the fog. Collier had been directed to a certain Methodist coastguard who would help him and with whom he was to lodge. A handful of country folk living on the sea-coast with a strong "church" influence in their midst, the arctic condition of the weather, the evangelist himself a complete stranger to every one, Method-ists included—were ever conditions more un-favourable to an evangelistic Mission? . . .

At the end of his year in Kent Collier was appointed to a ' circuit,' which signifies, in the Methodist dialect, a group of churches worked conjointly by one, two, or more ministers, assisted by a staff of voluntary lay preachers.  Collier's circuit was Brentford, in Middlesex, which included within its boundaries Twickenham and Hounslow. Here his next three years (1882-1885) were spent —the first two at Twickenham, the last at Hounslow. Unfortunately, the record of these years is almost a complete blank.  Of no period of his life since he left home to go to school do we know so little. Personal documents there are none ;  not a single letter remains, and the journal which had been kept with such conscientious detail in Kent was not resumed.  In 1884 a somewhat serious illness proved the opportunity for a holiday of several weeks in Switzerland, where a rough kind of diary was kept, but it tails off rather badly, and even at its best is little more than a somewhat colourless catalogue of the usual things which are seen and done by every Swiss tourist.  Collier was never the kind of man to write a *Journal Intime* ;  he had none of that genius for self-revelation which lightens so materially the task of a biographer, and at the same time enhances so greatly the joy of the reader.

The interest of these three years, then, lies almost exclusively in the opportunity which they gave Collier of putting into practice and testing some of his theories of successful church work.  The circuit system, as it was then worked, made a continuous ministry in the same pulpit impossible : the young man had to take his turn with his senior colleagues. He resolved, therefore, to see what could be done by thorough and systematic methods of pastoral visitation. A little note-book lies before me now in which he entered, not only the names and addresses of his people, but all manner of personal and domestic details that might be of service to him as he went on his rounds—the father's occupation, the names of the children, recent family sorrows, and such like. Not only so, he taught and trained a large band of workers to share with him the responsibility of ministering to the spiritual needs of their own neighbourhood ; and he did it in this way. Finding it impossible to be in his own pulpit regularly on Sunday evenings, in consequence of the claims of other parts of the circuit, he made a bargain with his Superintendent : ' Give me,' he said, ' one night a week which I can call mine.' It was done. Then he invited all those who were prepared to join in a bit of definite aggressive evangelism to meet with him on that night. At the first meeting twelve were present. He told them that he should always be there on that night for prayer and praise, and for conference on Christian work. The numbers grew steadily until they reached nearly a hundred, and on them, according to their willingness and ability, he laid tasks of Christian service. ' No time is better spent,' he told his ministerial brethren from the

Chair of the Plymouth Conference in 1913, ' than that in training workers.'

' But,' he went on, ' it requires great patience and persistency. Teach them to visit, to conduct cottage-meetings and lodging-house services, to lead sinners to Christ, to conduct clubs for the young, to work in the Sunday School, to engage in all kinds of Christian and philanthropic work. Gather them together, so that you may collect all the results of their work as information for yourself in your work. You will multiply yourself again and again by this means, and enlarge your influence beyond your dreams. To leave a band of devoted workers in a circuit, men and women who were idle when you entered the circuit and are now busy for God, is to have accomplished lasting good.'

In saying this it was probably his old Twickenham and Hounslow days that he had in mind. Elsewhere [1] he has told in greater detail how he put his own counsels into practice. The methods adopted, he says, ' when I had to face the problem of filling a circuit chapel and make my first attempt at church organisation,' were as follows :—

' 1. The whole district was canvassed three times within the first month. The workers met to supply me with all the information that they had gathered about non-worshippers, lapsed worshippers, children who did not attend Sunday School, the social conditions of the people, etc.
' 2. To those who had been able to undertake this special canvass an appeal was made for

[1] In a foreword to a little pamphlet, *The Christian Workers' Association,* by John Hugh Morgan.

visitors who could visit regularly ten, twenty, or thirty houses weekly.

'3. An arrangement was made to meet them, at first once a fortnight, and afterwards once a month, to train by suggestion, to receive reports, and to keep in touch with the sick, poor, non-worshippers, newcomers into the district, etc.

'4. A "Button-holing Brigade" was formed to invite loiterers in the neighbourhood of the chapel during the half-hour before the service.

'5. Suitable officials were stationed in the porch and aisles to act as welcomers to strangers.

'6. The chapel was divided into sections, and over each section a worker was appointed to welcome strangers, and to secure their names and addresses, which were handed to the minister at a special meeting on the Monday night.

'7. Sections of work—open-air and cottage services, relief, and other evangelical and social agencies—were formed.

'8. All sections of the work were combined in a Christian Workers' Association. The workers were invited to meet after the prayer-meeting on the Monday night, and especially at the appointed meeting of the Association held at first fortnightly, and afterwards monthly.'

Such were the methods employed, and by means of them, Collier himself declared, the chapel of which he had special charge was filled in three months, though he had only three Sunday appointments during that time. Nor was he ever moved from his purpose by those who, hearing as they thought the clatter of too much machinery, raised the old cry of ' over-organisation.' ' I am tired,' he told the Conference, in the address which has already been quoted, ' of the cry that we are over-organised.'

' Many churches are badly organised; they are busy and bustling, the programme is full of all sorts of efforts without any unity of aim, without any controlling hand, without any centrality of purpose, everybody doing that which is right in his own eyes, sections clashing with each other, work without system. That is not *over*-organisation; it is either faulty organisation or else failure to organise. What is needed is the gathering of all sections into one association of workers, under the sympathetic guidance and wise control of the minister as leader.'

There are those still living who recall with enthusiasm the stir which the young Methodist preacher—he was still only in his twenties—made in the dull and decorous round of their church life. Nor was it only among his own folk that he attained a good report. At his farewell meeting the local Roman Catholic priest was one of the crowd which filled the church to overflowing, to testify by his presence his appreciation of Collier and his work. But too much must not be made of all this. It is always easy to ' think the rustic cackle of your bourg the murmur of the world.' Thus far Collier had been only trying his wings; the long and perilous flight which should really test and reveal his powers was still to come. He had shown unmistakable gifts of initiative and leadership, but only in a narrow and limited field. He was still an unknown man. The Brentford years had not brought him fame; they had done a better thing —they had enabled him to take the measure of the problems to be solved, and they had revealed to him the lines along which he could best make his own contribution to their solution. It was not Collier's way in after years to overrate this first chapter in his ministerial life. Sometimes, indeed, he spoke as if he judged it something of a failure. It was not that; neither was it of a kind to call for record or comment to-day, were it not for what came after. Kent, Twickenham, and Hounslow were but stages on the road to Manchester, where he was to find the work which he came into the world to do.

# CHAPTER III

## THE MANCHESTER MISSION

### 1885–1921

THIS is the third chapter of our story. Yet in a very real sense the life of Collier has only one chapter : its name is ' Manchester,' and it is thirty-six years long. It began when he was within a month of his thirtieth birthday, and it ended with his death in June 1921. Any attempt to write in orderly sequence the story of these years would resolve itself into writing the history of the Manchester Mission, with which, from this point onwards, Collier's life is inextricably intertwined. But in this chapter we are concerned with the Mission only in so far as it serves to reveal the man. Moreover, not a little of the relevant material will be more conveniently distributed over the chapters which follow, in which an attempt is made to bring out various aspects of his character and work. Even so what remains, and is strictly pertinent to the story of the life, will require a chapter of such disproportionate size that it will be well to break it up into a number of smaller sub-sections.

## I. HOW THE MISSION BEGAN

' After preaching at Congleton, Macclesfield, and Stockport in my way,'—so runs the entry in Wesley's *Journal* on March 30, 1781—' I opened the new chapel at Manchester, about the size of that in London.[1] The whole congregation behaved with the utmost seriousness. I trust much good will be done in this place.' The following Sunday, he goes on, ' I began reading prayers at ten o'clock. Our country friends flocked in from all sides. At the Communion was such a sight as I am persuaded was never seen at Manchester before : eleven or twelve hundred communicants at once, and all of them fearing God.' The scene was repeated several times in Wesley's experience—in May 1783, in April 1784, and again on Easter Sunday, 1790, when, he says, ' I think we had about one thousand six hundred communicants.' And during a great part of the next century the chapel maintained the glory of its early days. When it was first opened, we are told, it was thought by many to be ' too much in the country ' (!). But the green fields soon became only a memory ; a vast new population sprang up ; the great chapel over which Wesley had rejoiced was crowded regularly with worshippers. It is even said that at one time ' a sitting could not be secured unless the applicant

---

[1] A picture of these two famous old sanctuaries—City Road, London, and Oldham Street, Manchester—may be seen in the ' Standard Edition of the *Journal,* vol. vi. p. 145.

was content to wait for months and even years.'
' Oldham Street, Manchester,' came to be generally
recognised as the headquarters of Lancashire
Methodism. But as the century wore on, changes
which have affected so profoundly the central areas
of our large towns began to tell their tale here also.
Gradually, as the population grew and commerce
prospered, warehouses took the place of homes ;
the business man no longer lived over the shop ;
he worked in the city, but he lived in the suburbs.
And so, one by one, the old families moved out,
while very few moved in to take their place. There
is no need to dwell upon what is so familiar to all
who have watched the development of modern
city life ; it is enough to say that, a hundred years
after its triumphant opening by Wesley, Oldham
Street Chapel lay derelict. The huge Sunday congregations had dwindled to a tiny handful of fifty
or a hundred. Scores of young and prosperous
churches had, it is true, sprung up which looked to
Oldham Street as their mother church ; but she
herself lingered on in a feeble and inglorious old
age. What was to be done ?

One thing was clear : it was impossible, as
Dr. H. J. Pope said, to defend the retention of so
costly a site in the business centre of a great city,
unless it could be put to some better use. The
chapel was rarely opened except on Sundays, and
then only for the benefit of a few devout souls who
might quite easily have been provided for elsewhere.
Under the circumstances it is no wonder that from

time to time proposals were made for the sale of the property and the use of the proceeds in the erection of new churches in new suburban areas. But, as Dr. Pope justly argued, there is one thing worse than the sight of an empty chapel in a crowded neighbourhood, and that is the sale of the property and the abandonment of the work. And when the money so acquired is used for the benefit of people who are well able to provide for themselves, the humiliation is complete. Fortunately, bolder and wiser counsels prevailed. A few far-seeing men saw in the derelict old chapel an opportunity for Methodism to attempt its old work under new conditions; and in the end their advice to retain the site and to rebuild the property was acted upon. This decision, it is not too much to say, marks one of the turning points in the history of modern Methodism. It checked decisively that facile and fatal policy of abandoning the centres of great cities which has become so grave a reproach to Protestant Christianity alike in the old world and the new.

The closing services of the old chapel were held on Thursday, February 1, 1883. They were conducted, in the morning, by Dr. W. B. Pope—Collier's old theological tutor at Didsbury—and, in the evening, by the Rev. Charles Garrett, the President of the Conference of that year. Taking as his text Psalm cxlv. 4, 5, which he read from the old Bible that Wesley used at the first service in the chapel, Dr. Pope said—I quote from the

report in the *Manchester Guardian* of the next
day :—

'The sentiment of the day was a mingled one,
in which the memory of the past and the hope
of the future strangely mingled. Those final
services were burdened with the weight of an
entire century of most hallowed recollections,
enough, if justice could be done them, to impress
on the present gathering a character of unspeak-
able pathos. But while they must needs yield
themselves to reflections that saddened their
departure from that time-honoured building,
they were comforted—more than comforted,
they were inspired—by the thought of the future
awaiting them in another building which was
not another but the same, where the glory of the
old house would reappear, as they believed, in
augmented brightness. Like the Jewish fathers
in the days of Nehemiah they remembered the
former house and might weep ; but like the
children of those fathers they rejoiced over the
new foundation. The two voices of sorrow and
of joy blended indistinguishably, but the sound
of the rejoicing predominated now as it did
then ; and, as in the old scene, would be heard
afar off, in the present case to the utmost skirts
of the religious community which they represented. They paid their tribute to the generations gone, who had spent their lives and their
devotions there; but they purposed to continue
both their devotions and their work, transmit-
ting all with increase to the generations that
should be born. In that hope they were greatly
solaced, and should go on their way, sorrowful,
indeed, that they would see that place no more,
but always rejoicing because they would find
its sanctities renewed in another if not a better
place.'

The memorial stones of the new building were laid, after many disappointing and vexatious delays, in May 1885.

In all these discussions and arrangements, it should be clearly understood, Collier himself had not the smallest share. He was still quietly at work at his post in the south, knowing no more, probably, of the new Methodist policy in Manchester than its promoters knew of him. Not until the Conference of 1885 was the first link forged between him and the future Mission. His connection with Manchester came about in this way. During the period of reconstruction it was necessary, of course, to make some provision for the small remnant of the old Oldham Street church and congregation. Sunday services were held in the Lever Street Sunday School hard by, and a young minister was appointed to shepherd the little flock until the new fold was ready for its reception. The minister in charge was leaving at the Conference of 1885, and Collier was invited to become his successor. At first he declined; subsequently, however, he agreed to leave himself in the hands of his brethren, with the result that in September of that year he found himself the pastor of a little Methodist society numbering about forty-five members and having its temporary home in the Lever Street School.

It is easy to understand Collier's reluctance to take up this new task. What possible attraction could it have for him or for any man? It was not the difficulties of the situation that daunted him. The dingy premises, the depressed remnant—if these had been all, a man of his mettle might have found in them both a challenge and an opportunity. But the hard, cold fact, which Collier quite well understood, was that he was neither invited nor wanted for more than one year. All that the Oldham Street trustees at that moment were looking for was some one who would keep things going during the year that still remained before the new building could be ready. It is important that this should be made clear, because in later years it was often assumed, even in Methodist circles, that Collier's invitation to Manchester was from the first an invitation to become the super-intendent of the new Mission. It is certain that nothing of the kind was ever contemplated by any one, and least of all by Collier himself. What was there, then, either of challenge or opportunity in an invitation to become a twelve-months' stop-gap ? Apparently, what served to reconcile Collier to a rather thankless and unenviable task was a brief revival of his old scholastic dreams. In his Dids-bury days, as we have seen, he had passed the ' Inter Arts ' examination of London University, and the prospect of a year in Manchester suggested the possibility of completing his degree. With that end in view he took rooms in Rumford Street, near Owens College, as it then was, and enrolled himself as one of its students.

Then straightway he fell to work on his one year's

task with a sublime forgetfulness of everything—
university classes or Oldham Street committees—
save the needs of Lever Street and its neighbourhood. His first Sunday was not encouraging :
there were thirty-eight at the morning service.
On the previous Sunday, when the congregation
numbered thirty-two, an old friend—the Rev.
G. Beesley Austin—had been in the pulpit and had
spoken loud in the new minister's praise. Collier
used to say that he owed the extra six to his friend's
advertisement. But he lost no time in putting
into practice the lessons he had learned at Twickenham and Hounslow. That first Sunday evening
saw him on the streets with a little band of Sunday
School teachers whom already he had managed
to infect with his own eager spirit. The officials
of the school seem to have been rather shy of the
new man and his new ways, and, if report be true,
sometimes treated him in rather cavalier fashion.
It made no difference ; week after week he was
there, and week after week he gathered fresh
recruits for his aggressive campaign. Nor were
his activities confined to Sunday. He visited from
house to house in the crowded areas round Lever
Street. He held Saturday afternoon open-air services for children, in the hope that through them
he might be able to reach their parents. He raided
the public-houses, and set up his first Men's Club
by way of an alternative. Often he walked the
streets of the neighbourhood till midnight, that he
might see for himself all aspects of the problem

which he was there, first, to understand and then to solve.[1]   And so, gradually, the cloud at Lever Street began to lift.   Officials dropped their shyness ;  the depressed remnant took heart again ; even the people around began to feel that a new light was shining in the all-prevailing greyness.

Meanwhile what had become of the studies and classes at Owens College ?   Once more, and this time finally, that door was closed against him, and by his own hand.   Whittier's noble lines about the American Sumner tell, with the change of a single word, exactly how Collier felt :—

> ' No trumpet sounded in his ear,
>     He saw not Sinai's cloud and flame,
> But never yet to Hebrew seer
>     A clearer voice of duty came.
>
> God said : " Break thou these yokes ; undo
>     These heavy burdens.   I ordain
> A work to last thy whole life through,
>     A ministry of strife and pain.
>
> Forego thy dreams of lettered ease,
>     Put thou the scholar's promise by,
> The needs of man are more than these."
>     He heard, and answered : " Here am I ! " '

Then the unexpected happened.   The year during which things were to be ' kept going ' was coming to an end ;  the great new building across the way was fast approaching completion ;  the time had come for selecting the man who was to lead the new enterprise.   To the amazement of everybody

[1] It deserves to be mentioned, if only in a footnote, that when he was out on these midnight expeditions a kindly landlady used to sit up for him and prepare a meal for his return.

the post was offered to Collier. The choice needs
no justification to-day, but it needed some courage
even to suggest it in 1886. It must be remembered
that Collier was still a young and unknown man ;
that Methodism was only just embarking, and that
somewhat timorously, on a new evangelistic policy ;
that it had laid out nearly £40,000 on this first
experiment ; and that failure here would have
meant discouragement, and perhaps even disaster,
along the whole line. It was no wonder, therefore,
that many of the leaders of the ' Forward Movement,' as it was called, were both alarmed and
indignant at what seemed to them Manchester's
rash and ill-considered choice. The man who was
mainly responsible for Collier's appointment, it is
now well known, was Dr. Henry J. Pope. Dr. Pope
was one of the most prescient Christian leaders of
his day, with an almost uncanny shrewdness in
judging men. Collier, whose admiration for him
knew no bounds, used to speak of him as perhaps
God's greatest gift to the Methodism of his generation.[1] While the younger man was busy about
his work, little suspecting what was in store for
him, the older man was watching and weighing,
and before the year was out had made up his mind.
Then very soon—as so often happened where
Dr. Pope was concerned—many others began to
discover that they also had made up their minds,

[1] At the Conference after Dr. Pope's death, Collier tried to speak at
the usual Memorial Service. He got through a few sentences, then his
emotion overcame him so completely that he was compelled to sit down.

that on the whole they agreed with Dr. Pope, that, in short, Collier was the man for the Mission. It is a curious illustration of how little Collier himself was anticipating the responsibility that was thus thrust upon him that he had intended, when his year at Lever Street was up, to accept an invitation which he had reason to know was being sent to him by the Methodists of Chorlton-cum-Hardy, but which in some way or other Dr. Pope managed to intercept.

Through the first five years of his ministry Collier had proved himself faithful in a few things ; he was now to be made ruler over many things. The best reward of work well done is the opportunity for more work, and of that reward, henceforth and to the end, he was to taste to the full. But though his sphere of service was thus so suddenly and so vastly widened, he did not forget that he still served the same Lord. When, on the Sunday evening of October 24, 1886, Collier preached his last sermon at Lever Street, he chose for his text 1 Sam. vii. 12 : *Then Samuel took a stone, and set it between Mizpah and Shen, and called the name of it Ebenezer, saying, Hitherto hath the Lord helped us.* Hitherto—in Kent, at Twickenham, at Hounslow, at Lever Street—he knew he had been helped, helped from on high ; and as he stood on the edge of the unknown land which lay before him, which he had never sought but which he must now enter, this was his confidence, that that help would not fail him. And it did not. The following Wednesday (October 27), the new building in Oldham Street—henceforth to be known as the Central Hall—was formally opened for public worship by the President of the Conference (Dr. Robert Newton Young). Further special services, conducted by distinguished ministers of the Church, followed, and it was not until the second Sunday of November that Collier began what was destined to be the longest continuous ministry in the history of Methodism. On the opening Sundays the fame of the preachers and the interest of the occasion naturally drew enormous throngs to the Hall; but there were many gloomy prophecies of what would happen when the special preachers had gone their way. It was even suggested that, since it was obviously impossible that the young missioner could attend to the details of organisation and minister regularly to the same congregation, he should be assisted, especially at the evening service, by men of mark and power; and tentative arrangements were actually made with that end in view. But Collier's first services put all the prophets to confusion; the ' star ' preachers were never called in.

It is interesting and significant to know that for his first Sunday evening sermon in the new hall, Collier fell back upon his favourite theme, *Able to save to the uttermost*.[1] It was not merely, as all preachers at least will readily understand,

[1] See p. 17.

that he wanted for such an occasion a subject with which he was thoroughly familiar; the text, as he interpreted it, enshrined the deepest conviction of his soul, the one thing which he had come to Manchester to say, and which the Central Hall Mission was established to make good. Christianity, some one has said, is ' the religion of all poor devils '; but the word spoken in scorn Collier would have hailed with rejoicing. It was exactly that, he believed, which was given him to proclaim : a gospel for ' all poor devils,' another chance for those who thought they had gambled away their last, love without stint for those whom no man regarded, *salvation to the uttermost*.

## II. HOW THE MISSION GREW

It is necessary again to remind the reader that these pages are the record of a man, not the history of a movement, and that much that would fittingly find a place in the one must be omitted from the other. Here there is room only for the barest outline of the rapid expansion of the Mission's activities which marked the next few years. Collier knew that in work of this kind the thing to be feared, and in all possible ways to be fought against, is the sense of staleness which is so apt to creep over the workers when the romance of a new enterprise has begun to fade. He made it a rule, therefore—and until the Great War laid its arrest on the whole life of the nation, the rule was pretty regularly observed—to make some new advance, some fresh development, every year. Twelve months after the opening of the Central Hall, the crowds at the evening service were so great that the St. James's Theatre, Oxford Street, was secured for a second service.[1] Two years later (in 1889) the great Free Trade Hall became available for the work of the Mission, and there every Sunday night, for the next twenty-one years, Collier ministered to what was often, and rightly, described as ' the largest Methodist congregation in the world.' At the end of that time (in 1910) a new and permanent home was provided by the erection of the Albert Hall in Peter Street. In the meantime, a number of old and well-nigh deserted sanctuaries in the centre of the city were detached from the circuits to which they belonged and brought within the Mission organisation, in the hope that they might share its more vigorous life. In only one instance was the hope disappointed. In some cases the old property was rebuilt or remodelled ; new workers with new methods were installed ; the house of God became again the people's home. Indeed, so swift and strong was the returning tide, that in 1904—I quote from one of the annual reports picked up at random—Collier was able to announce that the attendances at the various Sunday services of the

---

[1] Not, however, at exactly the same hour. It is an illustration of Collier's almost unfailing foresight in matters of detail that when in this way he arranged for double services, he always began one a little later than the other, in order that those who failed to gain admission at the first might be in time for the second.

Mission numbered not less than 16,000, independent of the still larger number that were reached every week by house-to-house visitation, open-air and lodging-house services, and other means.[1]

And then, alongside this intense religious activity, there sprang up, as the years went by, a vast network of agencies—the Men's Home and Labour Yard, the Women's Home, the Maternity Home and Hospital, the Cripples' Guilds, etc.—for the relief of the destitute and the repair of the broken. Of this part of Collier's work something will be said in a later chapter. At this point two things only need to be said about it. In the first place, as the later chapter will show, he began the social work of the Mission simply because he could not help himself; circumstances forced his hand. But reluctant as he must often have been—he was too clear-sighted not to know the perils which beset the path of the philanthropist—his judgment never wavered. Things being what they were, he could no other if he were to carry through the work which was laid on him to do. And, in the second place, it must be remembered that, to Collier's mind, the religious work and the social work were not two things, but only different aspects of the same thing. In other words, Collier was an evangelist, first, last, always, and in everything. All his labour was directed to one end—that he might bring men to God. If that is forgotten, the central fact is forgotten which explains all else. To speak

[1] See note on p. 67.

of him as an evangelist *and* half a dozen other things as well, as if evangelism were but one among many interests in a busy life, is entirely to mis-construe his work, at least as it presented itself to his own mind. To him it was all of a piece. Some of it might be done in a Sunday evening service, and some of it in the Men's Labour Yard ; that made no difference ; the work was one, and it was all, I repeat, the work of an evangelist.

The foregoing summary, altogether inadequate as it is, will give some idea of the scale of Collier's labours and of the success which they achieved. What were the principles which guided him ? Many of his methods have since been so freely adopted, both within and without Methodism, that much which, thirty-five years ago, seemed novel and startling is now familiar and accepted commonplace. None the less, it may be well to set down a few things which, if they do not explain the Mission's success, were at least things which Collier himself was wont to emphasise.

The building which took the place of the old Oldham Street Chapel, as we have already seen, was named, not a ' Chapel ' nor a ' Church,' but a ' Hall ' ; and not ' Wesley Hall,' as some would have liked to name it, but the ' Central Hall.' All which being interpreted meant that the Mission, though it was to be denominational, was not to be aggressively so. Its aim was not to persuade saints to change their ' ism,' but sinners to change their lives. It sought its constituency among those to whom all the Churches were as nothing, and the distinctions between the Churches as less than nothing. If those whom, through its agency, Divine grace rescued and redeemed elected to throw in their lot with the Methodist people, well and good ; but the Mission had no sectarian axe to grind. Especially was this true of its social work. ' Need, not creed,' was its motto ; nor was the fine saying, what mottoes sometimes are, merely a bit of coloured bunting at the masthead ; it was the rudder that steered the ship. As a writer in the *Manchester Guardian* happily put it, the social work of the Mission had made ' the world of want its parish.'

At one point the new Mission broke decisively with the traditions of the past. Several years before an attempt had been made, through an organisation known as the ' Manchester and Salford Lay Mission,' to minister to the spiritual needs of some of the poorest districts of the city. Nine small mission rooms had been opened and a number of lay agents appointed to work them. The results had not been encouraging. How indeed could it be otherwise ? When it is tacitly assumed that for the Christian worshipper there must be the best that architecture and music and a trained ministry can supply, but that for a ' mission ' all that is needed is good intentions and a warm heart, however shabby and incompetent the accessories may be, is it any marvel if the results are meagre ? The Manchester Mission changed all that ; and

when it is stated that the total value of the Mission
property to-day is not less than £250,000, and that
£25,000 a year is expended in carrying on its
manifold activities, we have a fair measure of the
greatness of the change. It was not the least of
Collier's services to the kingdom of God that he
helped to put an end to the era of the ' cheap '
mission.

Not less important was his linking together
unsectarian aggression and a due provision for
Church life. Here again there was a marked
divergence between the old methods and the new.
Before the mission was usually of the nature of a
' feeder ' to the local church—a sort of tender to
the big ship. Those whom it picked up it passed
on to be cared for and trained by others. At least
that was the theory, though it is to be feared it
often failed to be the fact. It is surely better on
every ground that young converts should remain,
wherever possible, in fellowship with those by whom
they have been led to Christ. But that involves
the thing upon which Collier laid such emphasis,
' the due provision for Church life,' and the old
methods did not make it. At the Central Hall
however, and at all the other centres of the Mission
a roll of Church membership was kept, classes
were formed for Christian fellowship, children were
taught in the Sunday Schools, men and women
were taught in Bible Classes, and the Sacraments
were administered, just as in any duly organised
Methodist Church. Let one set of figures speak for

themselves.   When the work of the Mission began it was not expected, even by warm supporters like Dr. H. J. Pope himself, that any considerable number of persons would be gathered into Church membership in Oldham Street.   The experience of later years in the old chapel seemed to forbid that.   Yet what are the facts ?   Here are the figures for the first nine years :—

| March. | Members. | Increase. | On Trial for Membership. |
|---|---|---|---|
| 1887 | 93 | 31 | 62 |
| 1888 | 183 | 90 | 91 |
| 1889 | 300 | 117 | 61 |
| 1890 [1] | 518 | 218 | 97 |
| 1891 | 777 | 259 | 163 |
| 1892 | 953 | 176 | 195 |
| 1893 | 1056 | 103 | 240 |
| 1894 [1] | 1317 | 261 | 333 |
| 1895 | 1484 | 167 | 345 |

Not only so, but in his Report for 1896 the Superintendent of the Mission declared that if ' the Conference sent an entirely new staff to take over the Manchester Mission next September, they would have no difficulty in finding every member returned, and would be comforted by the discovery of reserves quite sufficient to prevent the discouragement of decreases until they had got the reins well into their own hands.'   How much facts like these meant, not only for the strength and stability of the Mission, but for its effectiveness as

[1] In 1890, 156 members were received from two old chapels which were taken over by the Mission in that year. There was a further addition of the same kind of 102 in 1894.

a striking force in evangelistic operations, needs not to be pointed out.

Of Collier's tireless ingenuity in devising new ways of doing good, of the ceaseless vigilance with which the new converts were shepherded and cared for, and, above all, themselves were set to work, something is said elsewhere in this book. Before concluding this section, two further illustrations may be given of the large-minded way in which he interpreted his commission to do the work of an evangelist. Forty or fifty years ago that great word suggested to many little more than noisy ardour and narrow sympathies; but Collier filled it with new and nobler meanings. He knew that if men were to be won for God—and that, as I have said, was his aim in everything—they must be met upon their own ground. When, therefore, some years ago, the *Clarion* newspaper tried to rally the working men of England to the banner of unbelief, Collier, with the co-operation of Dr. James Hope Moulton, who was always one of the Mission's best friends, arranged two long series of Sunday afternoon lectures by well-known Christian apologists,[1] in order, not so much to controvert Robert Blatchford, as to demonstrate that it is still a reasonable thing to be a Christian believer. It was not the kind of work that Collier could have done himself, but no man understood better than he the importance of having it done, and he was

[1] Afterwards published under the titles *Is Christianity True?* and *What is Christianity?*

ready at all times to enlist the services of Christian scholars, in order that thereby he might widen the Mission's appeal to the men of his generation.

The other illustration is to be seen in the now famous Tuesday Mid-day Service which was begun in November 1886, and has been continued regularly ever since. Representatives of all the Free Churches and, during recent years, a steadily increasing number of Anglican clergymen have united to make this service as unique in the religious life of the city as perhaps it is in the religious life of the land. No part of Collier's work lay nearer to his heart than this, and on none did he spend more pains. He was always listening for any new voice that could speak with authority concerning the things of the Kingdom. If any man had a word from God to speak, and could speak it with power —provided always he was loyal to the Divine Lord—sooner or later he got his chance to speak it from Collier's platform. Dr. H. J. Pope used laughingly to say that if the archangel Gabriel were to visit this earth the first thing he would expect to hear would be that Collier had fixed him up to speak at the Central Hall! Few, probably, of those who joined with profit and delight in those mid-day services had any idea of the thought and care which had gone to the preparation of the programme. And this, too, was all of a piece with the one great purpose of the Mission. In the Men's Home Collier was striving to interpret Christ to poor, homeless vagabonds who were 'down and out'; in the mid-day service he was striving to interpret Him to the world of modern commerce.[1]

### III. HOW THE MISSION WAS FINANCED

Reference has already been made to the heavy cost of maintaining the Mission. With so many centres of work, both social and religious, and with a staff of paid agents—ministers, lay agents, sisters, nurses, matrons, secretaries, and others—numbering in all from thirty to forty, this was inevitable, even with the most rigid economy. Not less inevitable was it that the main responsibility for financing the big business fell upon the shoulders of the superintendent. It is easy to say that this ought not to have been, that the man who bore the burden of directing such an organisation should have been freed from the burden of finance. But in practice, as any one who has had experience in work of this kind is well aware, this is impossible. It is the man whom the public identifies with a cause who can best appeal in its behalf. For-

---

[1] Collier himself was almost invariably present at these services, and some of his comments on contemporary preachers and preaching were often well worth hearing. Only a fortnight before his death he said to a friend that he had noted this : that any man could lash the sins and follies of the world, but that to preach the Cross a man must live very near it. There is, perhaps, no harm in saying that, of all the men to whom he listened at the Central Hall, none impressed him so profoundly as Dr. G. A. Johnston Ross, now of Union Seminary, New York. He would gladly have incurred almost any expense in order to have secured his more frequent presence at the mid-day service. But Dr. Ross has been guilty all his life of hiding a very brilliant light under the bushel of an unconquerable modesty.

tunately, the members and congregations of the Mission were trained to give as well as to serve, so that out of the £25,000 which came to be needed annually for the work, £22,000 was raised within its own borders. Nevertheless, the remaining £3000, added to the special efforts involved in every fresh advance, laid a very heavy tax on Collier's time and strength. For example, the splendid Men's Home in Hood Street, Ancoats—probably one of the best of its kind in the country—meant an outlay of £25,000, and in connection with it Collier achieved one of his most spectacular triumphs as a money-raiser. In the spring of 1903 a great bazaar was held which raised in six short days the astonishing sum of £15,642. When the preparations for the bazaar began, Collier asked for £6500. Later on he raised the figure to £8500. He used afterwards to say that the good Manchester people got a little confused as to what exactly it was that he wanted, and so they gave him both.[1]

Collier had very definite convictions about the duty of the rich men of Manchester to the needy poor of their own city, nor did he ever think it necessary to apologise for putting their duty before

[1] The bazaar, it may be noticed in passing, was also the occasion of a tribute to the work of the Mission from the *Manchester Guardian* which was as generous as it was deserved : 'That success has come in a full tide, and in a tide which is still flowing'—the article appeared on the fourth day of the bazaar—'is a matter for congratulation beyond the bounds of the Wesleyan Methodist body, with which the Mission is more particularly identified. As has been pointed out more than once in these columns, the social work, which has its headquarters at the Central

them. The following characteristic little incident
is related by a well-known Manchester layman, a
member of Union Chapel—the chapel so long
associated with the ministry of Alexander M'Laren.
A meeting was being held there in 1919, in celebration of its fiftieth anniversary. The layman who
tells the story was giving some account of the
history of the chapel, and, incidentally, of some
of the wealthy and influential merchants whose
carriages used to be drawn up in a long line, Sunday
after Sunday, at the chapel gates. Among the
rest he mentioned one, a former M.P. for Salford,
of whom he said that at his death he left £2,000,000.
' Shame ! ' cried Collier, who chanced to be sitting
not far from the pulpit. Then followed a brief
colloquy between the man on the platform and the
man in the pew, which ended quite happily by the
speaker saying that if Collier had had anything
to do with Union Chapel at the time, it was
perfectly certain that Mr. —— would not have
been allowed to leave his two millions. Mr. W. J.
Crossley once told a Manchester audience that he
used occasionally to ask Collier to drink a cup of tea
with him, but that he had given it up, as he found

---

Hall, has made the world of want its parish. Its Homes and Shelters
for men and women, its prison-gate mission, its administration of
medical relief and sick-nursing, its maternity charity, its cripples' guild,
its home of rest—all these take account simply of human beings in need,
who are the charge, one way or another, of society at large. The noble
men and women who, day in and day out, are doing the work, zealously
but quietly, and with sober sympathy, are entitled, when they pause for
a moment to ask that their hands may be strengthened to receive a
response that shall not be too carefully calculated.'

that each cup cost him about £500 ! [1]   Sometimes a Sister of the Mission would take to the ' Super ' some peculiarly urgent and distressing case.  ' Jot down the details for me,' he would say, ' I am lunching with So-and-So at the Reform Club to-day.' A few hours later he would return with all that was needed.  When he invited a layman to take the chair at the great anniversary meeting in the Free Trade Hall he generally managed to make it quite clear that he was expected to contribute not less than, say, £200 to the anniversary fund. But in many cases there was no need to talk about money :  he had only to tell his story and the cheque-books came out.  One summer, when the Wesleyan Methodist Conference was meeting in Manchester, he took three wealthy laymen round the chief centres of the Mission.  Not a word was said about money, but afterwards—I tell the story on the authority of one of them—the three men put their heads together :  ' We ought to encourage work like this,' they said.  Each man agreed to write down on a slip of paper what he would give ; each man wrote ' £500.' [2]

---

[1] The same generous donor supplied the gas engine which was one of the costliest items in the outfit of the new Labour Yard in Hood Street. When the bill was asked for he sent it in with a footnote, ' subject to 100 per cent. discount.'

[2] Since the above paragraph was written I have received from the same Baptist layman another illustration of the unexpected ways in which money sometimes found its way into the coffers of the Mission. He received one day, he says, an anonymous letter from a Manchester citizen who had money to give away for charitable purposes, asking for his advice in the disposal of it, and stipulating only that the gift should be made in absolute secrecy.  This led him to a careful, personal

And apart from the character and quality of the work that was being done, men did not forget how tiny a fraction of the large sums which every year passed through Collier's hands found their way into his own pocket.  Everybody knew who knew him that had he gone into business, with gifts like his, and with far less labour than he put into the Mission, he might have been one of Manchester's merchant princes.  The late Sir Edward Tootal Broadhurst once said to a group of Methodist laymen : ' When you Methodists have done with Collier, let me have him ; I can find him work at a princely salary.'  And then I turn to the balance sheet of the first of the Mission's annual reports, and I find this entry under ' Payments ' :—

' By Minister's Stipend (1¼ years)    .    £187  10   0 '

Of course, this was in the early days of the Mission, when Collier was still a young, unmarried man ; but to the end he did his work on a stipend which, judged by the ordinary standards of commerce, was ludicrously small.  There is no need to dwell on the point, but men to whom he made his appeal, and with whom, had he cared, he might have had his place, remembered and responded.

examination of the work carried on under Collier's supervision, with the result that he advised his anonymous correspondent to give his money to the Manchester Mission.  Thereafter, every year, for six years, a registered letter, containing £50 in bank notes, was received, but without any trace of its source.  With the sixth instalment came a brief note saying that, owing to a change in the donor's financial position, and much to his regret, he was unable to continue the gift further. Collier was very greatly touched by the confidence alike of his Baptist friend and of the Mission's unknown and generous benefactor.

### IV. THE MISSION AS OTHERS SAW IT

It was only natural that methods of work so daring in their conception and so successful in their results should gradually compel the attention of social and religious workers in other churches and in other lands, and it would be easy to fill many pages of this volume with the tributes of those who, like Barnabas at Antioch, came and saw and were made glad. The judgment of Manchester's great daily paper has already been quoted. ' I am here,' said the Lord Mayor of Manchester (Mr. John Royle), on the opening day of the bazaar referred to in the last section, ' fearlessly to assert that I know of no institution in our city, or elsewhere, which is so admirably equipped for dealing with all classes of the needy, and helpless, and fallen. Nor am I acquainted with any benevolent institution which is better administered and more economically managed.' Dr. Moorhouse, the first of the three Bishops of Manchester who were Collier's contemporaries, was equally emphatic : ' I have never seen,' he said, ' an institution more adapted to help the destitute and to give self-respect to the fallen.' His successor, Bishop Knox, in sending to Collier a copy of his ' Charge to my Clergy '— ' though you, alas ! are not one of them '—wrote : ' I believe you will be so good as to accept it as a small token of brotherly kindness, and of my certainty that you in no way yield to any of us in your desire to make known the " glad tidings of reconciliation," but have been blessed abundantly in proclaiming them.' Bishop Temple, the last of the trio, only came to the diocese a few months before Collier's death, but he has been no whit behind his predecessors in the warmth and cordiality of his appreciation ; while Bishop Welldon, so many years the Dean of Manchester, wrote from the Deanery of Durham : ' I shall always think of him as probably the best exponent of practical Christianity in the great city to which he dedicated his life.' ' I am struck,' said Sir George Adam Smith, ' by the energy, inventiveness, the originality, and the sanity of your methods. May God raise up followers of your plans in every town in our country ! ' To Sir William Robertson Nicoll the Mission seemed ' the greatest piece of work that any church has accomplished in this generation.' Still more significant, perhaps, was the following letter from the Rev. Dr. S. Parkes Cadman, of Brooklyn, U.S.A. :—

' DEAR MR. COLLIER,—Will you allow me, as an outsider, and yet perhaps as one not altogether unacquainted with the work of your magnificent Mission, to express to you in this informal way the appreciation of many thousands of American clergymen, and of leading Christian workers in the United States, for what you have been able, under God, to accomplish in Manchester ? Your work is quoted in the Protestant Churches of North America as a model work, and as the most complete exposition of the evangelisation of a city in actual practice that we have to-day. . . . Sometimes Americans, generous as they are, have been surprised by the amount of money that you have been able to raise for this work, and the way in which you have led its developments from more to more has filled them with Christian joy. But when one makes a survey of it, and notes its strict business methods, its familiarity with the conditions of those it is meant to help, its combination of various qualities that are often absent from enterprises of this character, the only wonder is that you do not raise more than you do. We trust that you will maintain the happy balance characteristic of all that is done, and done so sanely and so well. To be institutional, social, in the best sense political, and always spiritual, without yielding in any appreciable degree to the weaknesses that beset these types, is to my thinking a triumph of Christian statesmanship; and when we remember the multitudes to whom you and your staff preach the Gospel in various ways, and with uniform faithfulness and success, our hearts are rejoiced, and we give thanks to God, the Giver of every good and perfect gift, because of you all.

'In behalf of my brethren, the clergymen of many American Churches, and myself,—I am, yours affectionately,

S. PARKES CADMAN.'

But perhaps the commendation which Collier himself prized most highly, and which, in Manchester at least, was of most real service to him, was that expressed again and again by Alexander M'Laren. In the 'eighties and 'nineties of the last century no Manchester citizen wielded a greater influence than the great Baptist preacher, and every ounce of it was thrown into Collier's scale. For years he attended regularly the anniversary meeting in the Free Trade Hall, and once even went so far as to say that if he had his years to live over again he would try to shape his ministry according to the pattern shown in the Manchester Mission.[1]

Yet all this, interesting as it is, is still but an inadequate measure of the widespread influence of Collier's life and work.  At the first meeting of the Mission Committee after his death a resolution was passed in which it was said that ' under his fostering care and inspiring leadership ' the Mission had grown to be both one of the chief centres of Manchester's religious life, and ' an object-lesson to Christian Churches in all parts of the world.' It was a bold claim to make, but it is justified by the facts.  Collier himself was always careful to avoid any attempt to thrust his own methods on others :  ' Work your own field according to its individual soil,' he used to say.  It is none the less true that fruit of his sowing is being reaped to-day in many churches and in many lands.  Dr. Johnston Ross once said that he could wish that every man who was seeking to enter the Christian ministry in England were ordered to spend some time within

[1] It was probably one of these meetings to which his biographer refers in the following note : ' He never perhaps took part in a meeting in the Free Trade Hall when the large building was not filled to its utmost capacity, and for years before the close of his career, almost invariably the immense audience rose to receive him and cheered enthusiastically Once, driving home from one of these meetings, his companion ventured to ask him if he could recall what his thoughts were as he stood waiting till the applause had ceased.  " Yes," he said, " perfectly; I all but heard the words, *It is a very small thing that I should be judged of you, or of man's judgment ; he that judgeth me is the Lord.*" '

the Mission watching and sharing in its operations ; and, as a glance at the Visitors' Book at the Men's Home will show, men did come from almost all Churches and all lands, in order that, as a distinguished Australian [1] once put it, they might be inoculated with the Collier lymph.'

## v. ' COLLIER'S MISSION '

' An institution,' says Emerson, ' is the lengthened shadow of one man.' That is eminently true of Collier and the Manchester Mission. He identified himself with it and gave himself to it in a quite extraordinary degree. He left to his colleagues a large and generous freedom in working out their own plans, yet just as a great editor somehow manages to make himself felt in every part of his journal, so did every part of the complicated organisation of the Mission bear witness to the deft and shaping touch of its leader. Never, surely, did any man live for one thing with a more consuming passion. He had few 'chums'; he had the Mission, and it had no rival. When well-meaning friends tried to lure him away into other work in which they were interested, he let them know, quite politely, but also quite definitely, that he was doing a great work and he could not come down. During the Great War he was invited to take charge of all the Y.M.C.A. operations in France. It was a great opportunity, and he would have risen to it. Moreover, there were no fewer than 2400 names

[1] Rev. Henry Howard.

E

—including those of his own four sons—on the
Mission Roll of Honour.[1]  But he dare not accept .
' The Mission could not do without me,' he said
simply.  And when, on his return from Australia
in 1921, he was urged to accept the Presidency of
the Free Church Council, again he declined.  His
sun was sloping to the west ; the few remaining
hours of daylight, he felt, must be given to the
Mission.

Yet in all this there was no ungenerous forgetful
ness of colleagues and fellow-workers.  He himsel
always objected when he heard people speak abou
' Collier's Mission.'  ' Collier's Mission,' he used t
say, ' won't last ; the Manchester Mission will.
Those who knew him will remember how ready h
was to efface himself, how little he cared for th
limelight, and how always he accepted whateve
public recognition was accorded him, not for him
self, but only as the representative of his staf
And it was right that it should be so, for never wa
a man served by a more loyal succession of co
leagues, both ministerial and lay, than was he
Yet they themselves would be the first to acknov
ledge that when the man on the street spoke abou
' Collier's Mission,' he was not really far wron;

[1] 350 of these never returned.

[2] It is impossible, of course, to name them here, but I shall be readi
forgiven, I know, if I make one exception in the case of the la
Jeremiah Sackett.  Mr. Sackett, who was considerably Collier's senic
was his lay assistant at Lever Street.  He went with him to the Cent
Hall, and remained by his side through many years, a man whose qu
strength carried many burdens for his ' chief,' and was repaid with son
thing like the affection and devotion of a son.

The Manchester Mission was, and remains to this day, the embodiment of the practical sagacity, inspired by love, which for thirty-six years Samuel Francis Collier consecrated to the service of the Kingdom of God.

## NOTE (p. 49).

In quoting these large figures some note may be taken of a criticism which was not unfrequently heard of the Mission, namely, that its congregations were 'too respectable,' that they were largely made up of men and women who, if they had not been in the Central Hall or Free Trade Hall, would have been in some other religious service. Statements of this kind are obviously difficult either to prove or to disprove. It may be granted that enthusiastic estimates of the Mission workers were sometimes as far out on the one side as those of their critics were on the other, and that many were to be found in the Mission congregations who belonged to the class of more or less regular church-goers. On the other hand, it must be remembered—(1) that to a certain extent the thing complained of was inevitable. Popular religious services, wherever they are held, always attract many besides those who are immediately sought. People go where people are; (2) that, after all, to be decently dressed is not one of the marks of the religious, or that, if it be, the very respectability' of the Mission congregations may be claimed as an outward and visible sign of the reality of the work done; and (3) that Collier himself was always alive to the peril of failure to get down low enough, and always contriving new plans to defeat it. For the rest, I am content to quote the testimony of a writer in the

Manchester *City News* who was present at one of the
Central Hall services in 1893 :—

> 'The speaker,' he says, 'had a unique and crowded
> congregation, the like of which I have seldom seen
> elsewhere. It consisted mainly of respectable artisans
> and their wives and families; present also were many
> of a lower order, from the ranks of unskilled and
> unsettled labour, nay, probably from the criminal
> class. To get some of the "roughs" present to attend
> in their ragged clothes was in itself a triumph, and
> there were women as well as men. Now it argues
> some devotion, the heroism of a convert, for a woman
> to show herself in shabby clothes on a Sunday night
> in a public assembly. It is at least a genuine sign.
> It is also to the credit of the Central Hall people that
> every one in the Hall attended on a footing of perfect
> equality; there were no reserved seats of any kind.'

# CHAPTER IV

## THE LOVER OF SOULS

AT this point it will be well to drop the slender thread of narrative in order to set forth some aspects of Collier's life and character as these were revealed during his thirty-six strenuous Manchester years. This may involve a certain degree of over-lapping, but it will help to secure a greater definiteness of impression. Half a dozen snapshots of the man while he is at his work will perhaps tell us more about him than any single portrait, however carefully executed, could do.

First of all, then, underlying and explaining all, Collier was a great lover, a lover of souls.

> ' I want an even strong desire,
> I want a calmly fervent zeal,
> To save poor souls out of the fire,
> To snatch them from the verge of hell—'

It was that passion, like a fire in their bones, which drove Wesley and Whitefield out into the highways and hedges of England in the eighteenth century, and it was the same passion which moved and wrought in S. F. Collier. Perhaps in nothing that he ever said did he manage to put so much of himself as in his address to the Pastoral Session of the Conference, and the following passage, so characteristic in its unadorned plainness and directness, uncovers for us the spring of all his activities :—

> ' John Wesley's dictum, " Your business is not to preach so many times, and to take care of this or that society, but to save as many souls as you can," has always been to me an inspiration and a law.  On entering the ministry, I was struck with the fact that the Methodist Church seemed to assert just the opposite.  To take the appointments on the plan, to dance attendance on members (they called it pastoral visitation) when there was no reason, to pay attention to the routine business of the society, all this seemed to be first, and if done, satisfied the Church.  The one work to which I felt called of God, and which Wesley put in the first place, *evangelism*, was the one work I found it most difficult to do.  I had to set my teeth with fixed determination in order to do this, the chief work of my life, and I have found it so every year since.  Everything calls for attention first ; every official and member seems content if other things are done, and it is the easiest thing in the world to find an excuse in the crowd of demands for failing to be aggressive, enthusiastic, successful, as a soul-winner. Brethren, we must put Wesley's words into practice, and to do this we must be prepared to pay the price.'

Words like these on Collier's lips must be given their full face value, for never, perhaps, did any Methodist preacher take Wesley's familiar counsel to heart more seriously than he did.  Everything

else he let go that he might win men.  We have
seen already how, first Heaton Mersey, and then
Lever Street, put an end to his dreams of a university degree.  And the same singleness of purpose
marked his whole life.  To the very end he took
little part in Conference, or in Synods, or on the
connexional committees of his Church.  Nobody
ever dreamed of calling him an ecclesiastical statesman.  True, he indulged in no easy scorn of those
who gave themselves to work of that order ; he
knew that in a highly-organised community like
that to which he belonged such work is necessary
if the machinery is to be kept running smoothly ;
but he knew, too, that it was not for him, and he left
it to others whose work it was.  On the other hand,
he could be very severe with the religious triflers
in the Church who expect their minister to be busy
about everything except his main business.  ' When
I went to my first circuit,' a colleague once heard
him say, ' I found myself in charge of a large, but
almost empty, church.  There was an immense
population all around, and I set myself to win them.
Many things claimed me and, had I surrendered
to their calls, would have prevented me from
accomplishing my main purpose.  Certain families
grumbled because I did not visit them ; one in
particular.  I would rather,' he added in an impatient aside, ' I would rather break stones than
dance attendance on people of that sort.  One day,'
he went on, ' I took my Bible and called on
this family.  I asked that all the members of the

household who could be spared should be called to-gether. When they had assembled I read a chapter. Then I said, "There is something I should like to say to you all." I had noticed that they only attended church once on Sundays, and I suggested that it would be a great help if they would try to be present at both services. Next I mentioned that I had heard that Miss —— (the eldest daughter in the family) had given up her Sunday school class. " I am very sorry to hear that," I said, " I am sure she ought to return." Then I knelt down and prayed. They never wanted me again. What they were anxious for was tea and gossip, not pastoral visitation.'

It should be understood, too, that when Collier said that evangelism was the one work to which he felt called of God, he meant something much more than the conducting of what are called ' evangelistic services.' Evangelism was for him, first of all, a personal obligation ; it was something which he owed not merely to a congregation but to A. B. and C. D. He carried the crowd on his heart, because he carried there the suffering, sinning men and women who make up the crowd. *Jesus findeth Philip . . . Philip findeth Nathanael :* there is no other way for Jesus to Nathanael but by way of Philip, and Collier was always ready to be Philip to some Nathanael. It is work like that which tests the strength and sincerity of a man's purpose. It was a great day in the life of the Baptist when there *went out unto him Jerusalem, and all Judæa, and all the region round about Jordan,* and he preached unto them, saying, *Repent ye; for the kingdom of heaven is at hand.* But the Baptist's supreme hour came when he faced the adulterous Herod in his palace alone and did not flinch : *It is not lawful for thee to have thy brother's wife.* Christ's philanthropy, as Robertson of Brighton once said, was no mere abstraction ; it was an aggregate of personal attachments : *Jesus loved Martha, and her sister, and Lazarus.* It is there where we so often fail. ' She would give,' Charlotte Brontë writes of one of her characters, ' in the readiest manner to people she had never seen— rather, however, to classes than to individuals. *Pour les pauvres,* she opened her purse freely ; against *the poor man,* as a rule, she kept it closed. In philanthropic schemes for the benefit of society at large she took a cheerful part : no private sorrow touched her.' But that was not Collier's way. He kept his compassion for the multitude fresh and strong, because he would not suffer the individual to be merged in the multitude. One of his frequent morning prayers, a Sister of the Mission says, was that God would send him some one that day whom he might help. ' I am increasingly impressed by the fact,' writes one of his old colleagues, ' that without " visiting " (in the usual sense) he had given scores of people the feeling that he was as interested in them as if there were no others on his mind.' The point is of so much importance for a right appreciation of Collier's work as an evangelist that it will be well to set down a little handful of facts in illustration of it.

In the early days of the Mission Collier used to pay surprise visits by night to the smoke-rooms and public-houses of the neighbourhood, in search of young men—sometimes the sons of worthy and well-to-do city families—who were beginning to play the fool. Even the public duties of his busy Presidential year brought no exemption from the claims of personal service. 'When he was President of the Conference,' writes one of his most intimate friends, 'he came home one evening, took in his hand a bundle of cards, and spent an hour working by himself through the queues outside the theatre doors in Peter Street, inviting the people to the Mission.' Here is a second incident of the same year. He arrived in one of our northern cities about mid-day ; he was the chief speaker at two enormous gatherings, afternoon and evening, and reached his home tired out after nine at night. There he met a boy, the son of his host, who had manifested a real concern about religion, and to him another half-hour was given in private talk and prayer. The decision registered that night, the father writes, still stands. The following is from a lady who served for several years as Collier's clerical secretary; and is best given in her own words : 'He expected utter devotion to the work from his staff, but to him we were human beings, not machines, and he took the trouble to understand us individually and to treat us accordingly.

At that time (1905) I was the youngest member on the staff, and as I look back now I realise how carefully he sought to guard me from the danger of too great familiarity with the material side of a great Christian organisation. He held himself responsible for me spiritually, and I have known him stop in the middle of dictating a batch of letters to ask me some personal question that seemed almost trivial, but the answer to which conveyed more than I knew at the time to his observant mind. Once he said to me, " I was lying awake thinking about you last night ; I 'm very anxious you shouldn't lose your keenness for spiritual things because you 're doing clerical work all day." I was amazed, knowing so well the endless demands made upon his thought and care, that he should have troubled about me personally ; but it was just those human touches that endeared him to us and brought the best out of us.' The simple truth is that where he judged the highest interests of others were concerned, Collier was never ' off duty.' During his later years he had a home at Deganwy, in North Wales. But even there, where he went for the rest it was impossible for him to get in Manchester, he must needs be up and doing. He interested himself in establishing a Sunday English service, and immediately set to work to gather a congregation on his usual Mission principle that people must be sought and found one by one. One man he visited eighteen times in vain, and was on the point of giving up in despair; but the nineteenth time he got him. Equally typical is a little incident which occurred on the return journey with Mrs. Collier from Australia, in the early weeks of 1921, the year of his death. They spent a few days *en route* in the south of France. At Monte Carlo Collier visited the Casino and watched the gamblers. He was particularly interested in observing a young married couple who had yielded to the fatal fascination of the play. Presently he saw them rise hurriedly from the table and overheard the husband say, ' Oh, my God! I 've lost everything; I 've lost £500.' At the moment nothing further happened, but again and again, afterwards, Collier reproached himself that he had not obeyed the impulse to speak to them. All through the night and repeatedly on the way home he was haunted by what he called ' My lost opportunity.'

Nor was there in all this the smallest touch of unreality or cant. I have failed altogether to show my friend as he was if anything that I have written has even faintly suggested that odious character, the religious busybody who delights to pester strangers with his unctuous impertinences. Collier's zeal never tired, but it never ran away with him; it was directed by as cool and sane a judgment as any Manchester merchant brought to the morning tasks of his city office. But things like those I have named show how steadily the wind blew from the same quarter, how deep and abiding was the love which moved him to seek by all means to save some. Indeed, there were few things that he dreaded more, for himself or for his fellow-workers, than that they should slip into the worn and shining grooves of Church routine, holding the appointed meetings, going the daily round, blind to the steady slackening of the central impulse. 'I remember,' one of the Sisters of the Mission writes, ' the first Sunday morning he came to preach at the Bridgewater Hall after my going there. He asked me how I was getting on. In telling him of the drinking among the women— a slum district was a new experience to me then— I was overwhelmed and the tears ran down my face. Putting his hand on my shoulder, he said : " Amy "—he always called us by name—" pray you may always keep that tender heart and never get hardened to the sin and need." '

And it was because he kept his own heart tender to the needs of others that men and women in need turned to him with such eager, pathetic confidence. Henry Drummond's biographer has told us how the large trust which his personality and his writings so magically produced made him, perhaps beyond any of his contemporaries, the father-confessor of multitudes of souls in religious perplexity. They were men and women of another type who turned to Collier; their sorrows sprang from a different root ; but they were not less sure that he could and would help them. Day after day the letters poured in upon him—letters from the ignorant, the poor, the maimed, the despairing ; letters from broken-hearted fathers and mothers, wives and sweethearts. 'More trouble, Gipsy,' he said one day to his friend Gipsy Smith, as he laid his hand on the usual morning pile, 'more trouble.' A small bundle of these letters, old and faded now, has been preserved, and one can still read between the lines the sad life histories of which they tell, and the love to which they make their appeal. One, for example, is about a fugitive from justice, whom Collier persuaded to give himself up and who was given a second chance. Another is a pencilled scrawl from a gaol-bird who had been twice sentenced to seven years' penal servitude : 'O sir, if you could only get me something to do, nothing would tempt me to go astray. I should like to let my friends see how different I could be. I am now in a miserable condition ; I wander about like a lost sheep. Try me, sir, and help me to get work, and with God's help I will be a credit to you, sir, and everybody around.' Another, the saddest of them all, is from a young girl : 'I am so young,' she says, 'only seventeen, and my life seems finished. I was very nearly drowning myself last Tuesday. I can never be the same again, and I was so happy. But don't turn against me, love me and pray for me.' And sometimes the appeal to pity and to save came not by post but in person. He was going down to his office one sombre, foggy Manchester morning ; on his way he passed, without noticing, two persons standing together in the gloom. Then a woman's voice called to him : ' Mr. Collier,' she said, ' you have done your best to help me ; you have tried to save me, and I 'm thankful to you for what you have done ; but there is no hope for me ; I am already in hell. But do you see this lassie ? ' she went on, pointing to her companion, ' she is only seventeen, and she is straight, and last night she drifted into the hell where I am, and she has no money and no friend. But she is straight, and you know what would have happened; so I gave up my living last night and slept with her, and I have come to you this morning to ask you, for the sake of what I once was, to save her.'

And this lover of souls, too, as Myers says of St. Paul, had souls for his hire. The little sheaf of letters from which I have been quoting contains not only appeals but glad, tearful responses. Some come from men and women in Canada and in the United States of America, whom he had helped to set on their feet, and who, in the language of their adopted country, were ' making good.' One is from the fugitive from justice referred to in the last paragraph who writes full of humble gratitude for all that had been done for him. ' I shall never forget,' says another, a minister's son, who had lost his place on the social ladder through his own wrongdoing and had been helped back again by the Men's Home—' I shall never forget how, when I was homeless, destitute, and friendless in Manchester, you held out the helping hand to me, how you placed me in the Home, and what an influence my residence there has had on my life. I dare not think had not God in His goodness guided me to you what might have happened.' One correspondent who is to take the chair at a Home Missionary Meeting, and wants some literature on the subject, adds in a postscript, ' I don't mind telling you that at one time I bought my clothes in Flat Iron Market,[1] but, praise God, His grace has worked a wonderful change in my life.' My last extract, which I give exactly as it stands, spelling, punctuation, and all, speaks for itself :—

> ' Mr. Collier,—Through gods grace. i must acknolage. hearing your sermain. in manchester. some six weekes ago. i have not only turned oveer. a new leafe. but christ. our evenly farther. has given mee a new book. for to comance my new and hapy life with.   i often get thrown from one side of the engine rom to the other. i wested (? used) for to utter a kurse. but now i thank god i can sing his praises.  i trust i may soon find employement where i can spend more time in gods worke. as it is the happyest. time i ever experienced in all my life.  the drink has been the ruine of my life and home. but christ has taken all my craven for it away.  i must now thank our hevenly farther for the paciance and kindness he has bestowed on a sinner as i have been.  god keep mee faithfull.  Sir your at liberty for to make this known. as i was a well known drunkerd. and a blastfeamer. in manchester.'

[1] A well-known rendezvous in Manchester where second-hand goods are offered for sale.

So did love bend low beneath his brother's burden,
hankful when the answer and the guerdon were
iven, yet not cast down when they were denied,

> ' Knowing one thing the sacredest and fairest—
> Knowing there is not anything but Love.'

# CHAPTER V

## THE WORKER

In trying to give some idea of Collier as a worker it
will be best to begin by describing his normal
working day. What is said elsewhere in these
pages will be enough to show how his Sundays
were spent. Morning, noon and night the services
went on—large and small, indoor and outdoor,
ordinary and special—almost without a break.
Yet Collier was often heard to say that for him
Sunday was the easiest day of the week. Every
morning, Monday included, he left home for his
office shortly after 8.30. At 9.30 he conducted
worship with the members of his staff. The rest
of the morning was spent answering letters, interviewing callers, consulting with colleagues, directing
and inspiring the ceaseless ' offensive ' which had
its ' General Headquarters ' at the Central Hall.
Whenever possible he took his mid-day meal at
home, returning to continue the work of the
morning until five or six. The evenings were almost
always taken up with meetings of one kind or
another, and he was rarely home until a late hour.
The Saturday nights of the winter saw him in
charge of the Popular Concert which was from the
first a conspicuous item in the Mission's weekly

programme. Ministers who manage to get at least a few quiet morning hours in the study with their books will know how to appreciate the sacrifice that all this involved. ' The books of a minister's study,' wrote one ministerial visitor after coming away from that busy room in the Central Hall, ' are more alluring than an office whose library consists of Mission Reports, and the memoranda of the various branches. It is sweeter to think quietly in the suburbs than to work long hours in a room to the click of typewriters, and to the constant ring of a telephone bell. The prospect from the office window is that of high buildings, and a smoky sky. The streets without ring to the slow beat of horses' feet, clanging as they pull the weighted lorries with their loads of cotton over the cobbled stones.' But Collier himself asked for no man's pity ; he was in the way of duty, and he cast no lingering looks behind.

It was every way characteristic of Collier that, as I have already said, he made no difference between Monday and the other days of the week. Many ministers whom no one would charge with laziness feel themselves fully at liberty to ' ease off ' a little as soon as Sunday is past. But Collier had an almost morbid horror of anything that might justify the lay suspicion of ministerial slackness. ' Mondayishness ' in his eyes was simply a bad habit which was not to be yielded to. ' If you must have a day off,' he said once, not very consistently, to the members of a ministers' meeting,

' take Tuesday, and so avoid the common gibe about ministerial Mondays.' ' Never advertise your recreations ' was another of his counsels in the same vein. And when he said these things his aim was both right and wise ; nevertheless, it sometimes led him to be unfair both to himself and to others. He seemed to forget that the business man whose stern application to duty was his daily judge had always his Sunday free, and often a half-day in addition, while he had only occasionally the one, and never, except during his brief holidays, the other. And Nature, as is her way, sent in the bill in the form of occasional and sometimes serious breakdowns in health. As early as 1888, when he had only been three years in Manchester, he had to go away on a long sea voyage to recruit. The marvel to many of his friends is not that he died worn out at sixty-six, but that under such constant and tremendous pressure his strength held out so long. But the ideal never relaxed its hold upon him ; again and again he would say, ' When I fail to put into my work as much time and thought as the best business man in Manchester puts into his business, it will be time to retire.' Nor did Manchester business men fail to recognise his tireless devotion. One of them once remarked to one of his colleagues that he believed in the type of Christianity that got a man up in the morning. ' I used to pass Collier,' he said, ' on my way to business every morning, and though I never spoke to him, the sight of him going as faithfully to his

work as I went to business impressed me very
much.'

It was, I suppose, this aspect of the man that
led one of his associates to speak about his ' ruthlessness.' 'He combined,' he says, ' the ruthlessness of the organiser with the emotional zeal of the
evangelist. Had he been a general in the army
he would not have spared his men, nor himself ;
he would have sought success in battle at any cost.'
And he goes on to compare him, in this respect,
with Florence Nightingale, who made slaves of all
who came under her command, and, blind to everything else save her own benevolent schemes, was
sometimes strangely unjust even to her most
devoted friends and servants. There is, perhaps,
a measure of truth in this. It is certainly not
surprising if some who lacked his driving power,
and could never go his pace, sometimes stood in
awe of his almost pitiless energy. Yet even though
they murmured they could never forget that, hard
as he worked them, he worked himself still harder.
Quite early in the history of the Mission one shrewd
observer noted, ' Collier never asks man or woman
to do work which he is not prepared to do himself.
He is quite as much at home at the head of a band-
march through the filthiest slums in Manchester,
or in a cottage service, or in house-to-house visitation, as he is on the platform of the Free Trade Hall,
or in the office of the Central Hall.' There, undoubtedly, was one secret of the immense amount
of work that was daily got through in the Mission :

Collier never spared himself, he was never merely a director of the work of others ; and if he was, as the old story of his boyhood suggested, very clever at getting other fellows to carry his parcels, it was always the heaviest pack that he kept for his own shoulders. Like Sir Walter Scott, he could 'toil terribly.' No smallest detail of his vast organisation seemed to escape him. A sentence from one of the annual reports of the Mission shows how the business man's ideal of unrelenting thoroughness pursued him in everything : ' All the results are carefully tabulated. Registers of all members and of all inquirers are kept with the promptitude and precision of a business house.' *Occupy—trade— till I come* was the Master's injunction to His servants, and this servant would accept no discharge from either advancing years or failing strength. In a brief, hasty note to his son Donald, dated May 13, 1911, and written when some throat trouble kept him out of the pulpit, he says : ' I am still resting at home. Mother says I am working hard. Well, I have to keep silent, and I must find other ways of serving the Master and extending His kingdom. Life is too short to be idle altogether. There is always a chance to be busy in some way or other for Christ.' But mere ' busyness ' accomplishes nothing ; like an unbanked stream it turns no mill-wheels, it grinds no man's corn ; it becomes of service only when there is behind it a strong, directing mind. And it was Collier's other gifts as a

worker that for him turned to gold his great gift
of industry.

(1) To begin with, his industry was yoked to a
very uncommon shrewdness. The title of one of
his addresses, which was at one time something
of a favourite with him, was ' Common-sense in
Christian Work ' ; and he was himself the very
embodiment of it. It came out in various ways.
For example, outsiders often expressed their astonishment at the apparent ease with which the
arrangements for the Tuesday Noon-day Services
and the great Anniversary Meetings were carried
through, and the regularity with which the money
poured in for the support of the manifold enterprises of the Mission. If they had had the least
glimpse of what went on behind the scenes, their
astonishment would have been modified. Nothing
was left to chance ; there were no last minute
arrangements—and, be it said, little mercy for
those who were content to make them—the results
attained were the results which had been long
and carefully worked for. Again, there was a
certain wiliness in the way in which, at a time when
some of his Mission methods had yet to win their
way to general recognition, he sometimes prepared
himself to propitiate hostile opinion. Where he
was fully convinced, he was not afraid to go ahead
alone, but as a matter of prudence he would sometimes quietly make sure of the good-will of men
who were not directly responsible for what he was
doing, but who could be counted on to stand by

him if opposition arose. To no man did he turn in such circumstances more confidently than to Dr. Henry J. Pope, and in none did he find a more loyal friend.

Collier was not a bit of a doctrinaire. Methods of work in his eyes were simply means to an end ; when they failed to get there he scrapped them without mercy. The Mission was there to save men, and, says one of his colleagues, ' he would have cast the whole organisation into the flames if it would generate heat to save one more soul.' ' If,' he said, in one of his informal talks to the members of his staff—' if you find any of your methods falling flat, or failing, don't continue to flog a dead horse. Never mind how successful the method has been in the past, leave it, cast it aside and expect God to give you a new idea with which to meet the demand of the present. Prayer-fully think it out and go ahead.' There speaks the man ; an enthusiast—yes, but an enthusiast wary in his enthusiasm, making it always the servant of a cool and practised intelligence, fitting means to ends with that unerring instinct which, I suppose, usually goes along with the highest kind of general-ship. There was in Collier something akin to the ' ice sense ' which, it is said, some sea-captains have, which enables them to detect the neighbour-hood of icebergs which are indiscernible by any one else. He seemed to see how things were going while others were still groping in the dark, and—to change the figure—he had his ship trimmed to meet the new set of the tide. But this was more than instinct; it was as well the wisdom that is born of long and patient observation. Collier was always on the watch. A worker in one of the branches of the Mission says that whenever he went to take a service there he would leave home early in order to walk through the small, mean streets of the neighbourhood, and gather if he could new suggestions for his workers. So he moved from facts to theories, and from theories back again to facts, always with his eye on things as they are, and always fashioning his tools for the work they had to do.

(2) Another of Collier's characteristics as a worker was his ready resourcefulness, his ingenuity in devising new ways of doing good. Once in a staff meeting he prayed—and the prayer lived in a colleague's memory—'Lord, make us clever in Thy work.' Equally characteristic was his counsel, ' Work in ways unthought of.' That was what he himself was always doing. ' One of God's commercial travellers,' a religious journalist once called him; and no representative of a business house was ever more alive to his opportunities, more eager to break new ground and do new business, than the superintendent of the Manchester Mission. He was continually trying fresh experiments; if they succeeded, well and good; if they failed, or if their usefulness was quickly exhausted, he dropped them at once. The superintendent of one of the

other Central Missions of Methodism once laughingly complained that if he got hold of what he thought was a fresh idea in Christian work, he was sure to find that Collier was ahead of him with it. Two or three illustrations will best show how love first divined the need and then planned to minister to it.

One November, many years ago, during Manchester race-week, when the city streets were crowded late at night with multitudes of the very men whom the Mission laid itself out to win, Collier arranged a series of midnight mission services. He conducted each of them himself, and one who was with him throughout the week remembers to this day, with something like awe, how he prayed and pleaded and wrestled, as only he could, with the great motley throngs that, night after night, found their way to the Central Hall. In 1910, what St. Paul might have called ' a great door and effectual ' was opened to him by the erection, in Peter Street, of the Albert Hall and Aston Institute, perhaps the most perfectly planned and equipped Mission premises in the country. Various departments of work which had had their rallying point in the Free Trade Hall Sunday evening service, and which had hitherto been carried on amid the gravest inconveniences, were now provided for, together with the evening service itself, in the new buildings across the way. At once Collier's busy brain fell, like some strong-winged bird of prey, on the happy task of turning

his new opportunity to the best account. Never
satisfied with what was already being done, he
would spend hours in consultation with his workers,
trying to discover social and religious needs of the
complex community about them, for which no one
else had taken thought, and how best to meet them.
In this way—I pass over a host of more ordinary
agencies—special gatherings were arranged for street
hawkers and newsvendors and old ' cabbies '—a
collection of human oddities in entertaining whom
Collier was often at his best—and for the caretakers
of business premises in the neighbourhood ; a
room was set apart for hospital nurses ; there
were classes for the Chinese engaged in the city
laundries ; cards were hung in the neighbouring
hotels inviting the waiters, servants and porters
to the services of the Mission. Was there any
lonely, neglected corps in the great army of the
city's workers whose need Collier did not set himself to understand and to serve ? And so it continued to be to the very end of his life. Only the
Easter before he died he was talking over the
possibility of forming clubs for the employés in
the large business houses in the centre of the city,
and of opening a home of rest for the tired mothers
of Hulme, by the seashore at Deganwy. One of
the Sisters of the Mission who was with him for
a fortnight after his return from Australia says
that he was always more eager to talk about the
work than about his journey. Whatever subject
of conversation was started, he always came back,

sooner or later, to the same point—the Mission, the Mission : what could they do that they were not doing ? what could they do better that they were doing already ?

At the first Mission Anniversary meeting after Collier's death, the Rev. Henry Howard, of Australia, narrated a little incident which, trifling as it may be, shows how wherever he went the Mission was always on his heart. ' Just twelve months ago,' Mr. Howard said, ' we were waiting in Adelaide to receive the Rev. Samuel F. Collier, the representative of British Methodism. I knew how tired he would be, and what a great crowd was waiting for him, so I got the Commissioners of the railway to flag the train twenty miles down the line, for I thought he would like to meet first some one whom he knew. I got on to the train and looked down the corridor. There stood Collier looking through the window. Suddenly he turned and saw me. He began with no greeting ; this was what he said : " Howard, my Anniversary ; second Sunday in November 1921, morning, afternoon, and night ; Tuesday, Free Trade Hall public meeting in the evening." " All right, old man," I said, " that 's all right." " And now," he said, " how are you ? " '

' You see,' Mr. Howard went on, ' this Mission was on Collier's heart and mind all the time he was in Australia. His body was there, but his spirit was here. He carried the double burden. And that was what killed him—he never stood from under ; he bore the burden of the Mission

hrough all the trip and through all his public
appearances.' [1]

(3) Perhaps if Collier himself had been asked to
explain his success as a worker, he would have said
that it all lay in setting others to work. On nothing
did he insist more strongly. ' Duplicate yourselves,
duplicate yourselves,' he used to say to his colleagues. ' It is possible,' he said once, ' that the
man to whom you give a piece of work will not do
t as well as you would have done it, but remember
that you have made another worker.' There was
no hope, it seemed to him, of the Church ever
overtaking the vast irreligion of the world except
by an enormous increase of voluntary workers, and
he would have had every circuit in Methodism
organised on the lines of work for each member,
definite, chosen, assigned. Nor was it merely for
the sake of the outside world that he preached his
gospel of work; the converts themselves, he believed, needed it no less. What led to the starting
of the theatre services, only a year after the opening
of the Central Hall,[2] was not only the lack of room

[1] Something might have been said here about Collier's quickness to
profit by the experience of others. One Sunday evening, several years
after the beginning of the Manchester Mission, he was discovered, not-
withstanding his lay attire, in a North of England congregation where
an interesting little experiment in Christian work was being tried. He
admitted that he was there to spy out the land, and to see if there was
anything in the new method that he could either adopt or adapt. In
the same way, when the plans for the Albert Hall were taking shape, he
picked the brains of all the Mission-hall architects whose work he was
able to visit and examine. Indeed, wherever he went, his eyes were
always open, pencil and pad were always at hand, and Manchester was
the gainer.

[2] See p. 48.

for the overflowing crowds, it was lack of opportunity for the multiplying converts. ' I have been busy for the devil,' said one of the early converts ; ' if I am to go straight, I must have something to do for Jesus Christ.' There was no resisting an appeal like that, and Collier set himself to meet it in a score of different ways. ' It is our aim,' he wrote, in one of his earliest Reports, ' to train all young converts to work. Our volunteers find plenty to do, according to their gifts, in the choirs, orchestras, brass bands, open-air singing bands, button-holing and welcome brigades, pastoral staff, district visitation, Sunday schools, bands of hope, lodging-house and cottage meetings, and special mission efforts, etc.' At the end of the first year he said, ' Our staff consists of the minister, three paid missioners, and some hundreds of voluntary workers.' By 1904 the ' hundreds ' had grown to two thousand, in 1913 it stood at two thousand five hundred. One of them, whose quaint words Collier often used to quote, speaking for multitudes in the Mission besides himself, said one night in the weekly class-meeting, ' I used to be a liability ; now I am an asset.' [1]

---

[1] A striking collection of these class-meeting sayings might have been made if only there had been some Methodist Boswell at hand to report them. Here is one with a touch of unconscious splendour in it : A man whose youth and early manhood had been spent in evil ways, and who was converted through the instrumentality of the Mission, was giving his testimony one night. He had met an old drinking pal during the week who had chaffed him for turning pious : ' I 'll tell you what I said to him. " Bill," I says, " you know what I am " '—he was a lamplighter— ' " when I goes round turning out the lights, I looks back, and all the

(4) But of all Collier's gifts as a worker the thing in him at which—if for the moment I may speak in the first person—I wondered most, which rebuked and shamed me again and again, was his power to *walk and not faint*. I used to link him in my mind with George Adam Smith's interpretation of the great prophetic word. To *mount up with eagles*—that is much ; to *run and not be weary* —that is more ; but, most of all is it to *walk and not faint*. And Collier could do that. Anybody can get up a ' sprint ' for five minutes ; he could grind along the dusty road for a day and still not be spent. Professor W. Sellar, it is said, once remarked to Matthew Arnold, ' What a good man —— is.' ' Ah,' sighed Arnold back again, ' we were all so good at Rugby.' ' Yes,' retorted Sellar, ' but he kept it up.' And this is the thing at which we marvel, and for which we give God thanks, in Collier : not simply that he loved so greatly and planned so wisely, but that he ' kept it up,' and kept it up to the very end. He had learned how to plod and to keep his passion fresh. The bush burned and was unconsumed. Deissmann has a picturesque phrase in which he contrasts Paul with Philo : ' Philo,' he says, ' was a lighthouse, Paul was a volcano ' ; the one had to be trimmed and

road over which I 've been walking is all blackness, and that 's what my past life is like. I looks on in front and there 's a long row of twinkling lights to guide me, and that 's what the future is since I found Jesus." " Yes," says my friend, " but by and by you get to the last light and turn it out, and where are you then ?" "Then ?" says I, " why when the last lamp goes out it 's the dawn, and there ain't no need for lamps when the morning comes." '

kindled by his teachers, the other flared with inner fires. In Collier the inner fires never seemed to die down. He had the ' calmly fervent zeal,' the ' even strong desire ' of which Wesley sings. Some sputterings of the holy fire there are in us all ; in him it burned through all the years with a fixed and steady glow. ' Jackson,' he said to me one day in a characteristic outburst, ' the trouble with so many of our fellows is that they so soon lose their " fizz." ' But Collier never lost his ' fizz ' ; he never knew the ' uncourageous elder years ' [1] which come to so many who begin life with high and generous hopes. Wesley could remember hearing his father say to his mother about one of her children whom she was patiently trying to teach, ' How could you have the patience to tell that blockhead the same thing twenty times over ? ' ' Why,' answered Mrs. Wesley, ' if I had told him but nineteen times, I should have lost all my labour.' Collier belonged to the same patient school. ' It 's no good troubling,' he used to say, ' if you don't trouble enough ' ; and the maxim, as was usually the case with him, had his own practice behind it. In his first year's work at Lever Street, he called fifty-one times at a working-man's house before he persuaded him to come to the services. Collier was of that high company who can say, *Having received this ministry, we faint not*—we do not lose heart, we do not give up, *we faint not* : that is all, and how much it is !

[1] The phrase is used by Dowden of the later period of Wordsworth's life.

# CHAPTER VI

## THE CHIEF

In the communications which have reached me from those who at one time or other have served as Collier's younger colleagues in the work of the Mission, there are so many references to his gifts of leadership that room must be found for a chapter, however brief, on ' The Chief,' as they in their affectionate loyalty commonly styled him. And I cannot begin it better than with yet another quotation from his address to the Pastoral Session of the Conference :—

' It is said that the preachers' weekly meeting is non-existent in many circuits, in others is merely formal or a friendly chat over a smoke, and that a regular meeting of the preachers in a circuit, for prayer, spiritual fellowship, earnest conversation about the work of God, and mutual suggestion how best to carry it on, is becoming rare. If so, surely we are neglecting, not only what is a great privilege, but one of the most important factors for successful work. Many a minister has been saved from depression and inspired to new effort at such meetings. As a young minister in my first circuit I was greatly impressed the first week I met my superintendent for prayer, fellowship, and consultation. In the commercial world no partners in business or board of directors would neglect or undervalue their regular meeting for detailed consultation. Is the administration of a circuit less important ? We shall make one of the biggest blunders if we allow the weekly meeting of colleagues in a circuit or mission to die out or become a matter of form.'

This, again, is the word of experience. Collier's Tuesday morning meeting with his staff was in some ways the most important of the week. It was the nerve-centre of the whole organisation ; the council of war, in which the commander-in-chief and his generals reviewed both their victories and their defeats, and shaped new plans of campaign for the future. Occasionally, perhaps, a younger colleague would resent the inevitable interference with the morning hours of study, but on this point Collier was resolute ; and even those who obeyed most reluctantly then would probably admit now that he was right. Nowhere did their chief show to greater advantage. ' It is twenty-one years,' one man writes, ' since I attended the last staff meeting, but the inspiration is with me still. The insight into human nature those weekly meetings revealed was most arresting.' It was there that Collier let fall and repeated those counsels of shrewd, practical wisdom, several examples of which have already been given. Two others may be added. At the meeting following any special season—Christmas, Whitsuntide, or the Anniversary—the workers were all asked to pool their experience : what had they done which next time they could

do better? what had they done which had better
not have been done at all? 'Don't just think
you will alter this or that next time; you will
forget by then; make a note of it now.' Another
of his sayings which must, I think, have been a
favourite with him, has reached me in various forms,
but each with the true Collier hallmark upon it;
in substance it was this: 'If you have a disagreeable
duty to perform, begin the day by doing it; don't
carry that burden about with you while you are
busy with other things.'

It has been very interesting to notice how many
of those who once worked by Collier's side, when
they sat down to recall their own memories of him,
seemed almost instinctively to drop into metaphors
drawn from the world of generalship and strategy.
He had a touch, and more than a touch, of the true
Napoleonic quality. He could take in a difficult
situation, gauging both its difficulties and its
possibilities with the eye of a born strategist. He
was as daring as he was cautious, and as cautious
as he was daring. He never shrank from a difficult
task, but he was too good a general to throw men
away on a hopeless one. As we have seen, he knew
the importance of detail; nothing seemed to escape
him, however insignificant; but he never let himself be buried under it. He stood over his facts,
handling and ordering them with the quick eye and
sure grasp of a master. Perhaps the best evidence
of this genius for generalship is to be found in the
affectionate and enthusiastic loyalty of those who

worked with him. All who came into contact with the Mission, even though only as occasional visitors, noticed and were impressed by it. 'I have never seen a chief,' one layman writes, 'more beloved of his staff than he was'; and scores of letters which I have been privileged to read bear witness to the more than soldierlike devotion to him of his humblest fellow-worker. How was it won? One who was not a colleague can only answer the question very inadequately; he must be thankful if he does not miss the road altogether; but some things may be said.

It is quite certain that the affection with which Collier was regarded was due to no want of firmness. I hesitate to use a word like 'disciplinarian' of him; it suggests ideas which were wholly foreign to his nature; but when he judged it necessary he knew how to assert himself unmistakably; and woe to the man who stood in his path! One who was present and who remembers well both the incident and the man concerned sends me the following: 'The members of the Mission Committee were sitting at tea, the guests of one of their number, when the conversation turned to a burning political question of the hour on which Collier knew that those present were sharply divided. Very quietly he said, "Better let the matter alone." But one man persisted rather thoughtlessly in pressing his own point of view. The heavy hand of "the chief" was on him in a moment: "I must ask you, Mr. ——, to drop the subject at once; not another word, if you please." And not another word there was.' ' Collier,' adds my correspondent, with the glow with which he always recalls his old chief's memory, ' Collier was a king amongst men, anywhere, and at all times.'

The sin, I think, which he always found it least easy to forgive in a colleague was the sin of slackness, the sin of ' the unlit lamp and the ungirt loin,' as Browning calls it. I remember nothing which stirred him so deeply as the thought of men in the ministry who took their work lightly, who habitually did less than their best. On one occasion when he was interviewing a young minister who seemed a likely man for a vacancy on his staff, the young man expressed his fear that he was not ' big enough for the job.' ' All I want,' said Collier, ' is a man who will take off his coat and work. If you'll do that, I'll back you up and stand by you to the end, even though you make mistakes.' But if a man did not take his coat off, if he was disposed to lounge through his day in dressing-gown and slippers, he soon got a taste of that ' ruthlessness ' of which something was said in a former chapter. When, as of course sometimes happened, hard work and manifest unfitness went together, the chief's duty was as plain as for him it was painful and difficult, and those who knew Collier's tender heart will find it easy to believe that laymen on his Committee sometimes thought that he was not prompt enough in ' firing out the fools,' that he suffered a colleague's diligence to hide the multitude of the sins of his incompetence.

But at least this reluctance is sufficient to show that, strict even to sternness as was his sense of ministerial duty, there was nothing in Collier of the mere drill-sergeant and martinet. Like Abraham Lincoln he knew how to ease the tension of work with a jest, and to find relief for over-wrought nerves in a good story. Those who have seen Mr. Drinkwater's famous play, or have read Lord Charnwood's biography of the great American leader, will remember how sometimes, at the very height of a crisis, he would turn for relief to the quaint drolleries of Artemus Ward, the author who almost vied with Shakespeare in his affections, and how on one occasion he even held up the business of his Cabinet, while he amused himself and them with a reading from A. W.'s latest book. Collier had the same happy art, as a reminiscence of one of his lady clerical secretaries will show: It was the eve of the Mission Anniversary, and both of them had been driven and harassed to their wits' end. Collier went home about tea-time, and the secretary settled down to get letters typed ready for signature on his return later. ' I really felt,' she says, ' things were getting on top of me, and when the 'phone went, and I was told " the Super wants to speak to you," I seized my notebook in desperation expecting to hear, " Just take this down, will you ? " Instead, the familiar voice came through, " I say, would you rather be a dog

—an ordinary dog, I mean—or a dog with a broken tail ? " " Why, an ordinary dog, I suppose." " Well, I wouldn't," was the quick retort; " an ordinary dog has his day, but a dog with a broken tail has a week-end ! " Then followed a characteristically infectious guffaw, and before I could say a word more he had rung off. But I went back to the letters with a laugh on my lips, and the work went merrily to the end.'

Another of Collier's qualities as leader is revealed in a conversation with his friend, Gipsy Smith. ' Why are you so anxious,' said the Gipsy, ' to pull in this man and that and the other ? Why do you not take the place yourself ? ' ' Gipsy,' said Collier, ' I am out for the kingdom ; it is the kingdom that matters to me, and the moment I find a man who is a quarter of an inch bigger than I am, and can do the work better than I can, I am ready to get him his crowd, to hold his coat and back him, while he does it.' ' No self-seeking there,' said the Gipsy, when he reported the conversation to me. And he was right ; Collier was above that littleness. But there is more in the words than unselfishness : it is the instinct of the true leader that speaks in them. Is it not always one of the marks of leadership that it knows when and to whom to delegate ? And, on the other hand, is there anything that so surely reveals a man's unfitness to lead as the petty vanity that insists on keeping everything in its own hands ? Few men, I think, have understood that better than Collier did. ' What is the first condition of leadership ? ' he once asked his old friend, Samuel Chadwick. ' Well ? ' said Chadwick, knowing his friend's way, and that he had got his own answer ready when he put the question, ' Well ? ' ' Self-effacement, ' replied Collier emphatically. ' Some men,' he went on, ' are so possessed with the sense of their own importance that they never give others their opportunity, and so never make leaders.' But Collier always put his men on their own responsibility, urging and encouraging them to develop on their own lines. As one of them put it, he directed but he did not dominate them. Nobody, I imagine, ever heard him talk psychology after the fashion of to-day, but he was for all that a practical psychologist : he studied men and women ; he noted their limitations as well as their strength ; he tried to discover their natural bent, and then set them free to follow it. Young ministers who joined his staff, sometimes with only a year or two's experience behind them, were amazed again and again at the lavish confidence he reposed in them. ' If,' he said to one of them at their very first interview—' if you have any new ideas, don't hesitate to suggest them ; there are many things we have not yet discovered.'

This respect for other men's personality was native to Collier and showed itself in minor matters as well as greater. One illustration of it which left a very deep impression on the mind of the colleague concerned may be mentioned. When he returned from Australia he had made up his mind that the immediate responsibility for the Albert Hall Church and congregation, which he himself had borne for so long, must be placed in the hands of another, the Rev. H. G. Fiddick. Shortly after the transfer had been made—in May 1921—a service for the recognition of new members was held at the Hall. It had been arranged so that Collier himself could be present, his colleague naturally feeling that it was fitting that the new members should be received by him. He came, but he refused absolutely to take Mr. Fiddick's place; he told the congregation himself that he would join with them in the service, but that it was for their own minister to give to the new members the right hand of fellowship. In less than a month he was in his grave; but the impression made by his humility and self-effacement remains with his young colleague a possession for ever.

This large confidence in others was a policy not without its risks; but magnanimity can afford to take risks, and Collier faced them without fear. When he said, in words which have been already quoted, ' Take off your coat and I will stand by you even though you make mistakes,' he was not talking idly. Sincerity and hard work could always count on him, even when he did not agree with all they said and did. For example, he had at one time a colleague with strong socialist sympathies who was in charge of a large Brotherhood. The meetings were often reported in one of the local papers, which did nothing, we may be sure, to tone down the ' red ' in the missioner's socialism. Some of the Mission's supporters grew alarmed, and wrote angry letters of protest to the superintendent, threatening to withdraw their subscriptions, and so on. Collier managed to quiet their fears, but said nothing to his colleague until the latter, hearing incidentally what had happened, expressed to his chief his regret for the worry he had caused him. He only said, ' I have bigger troubles than that, my lad ; you go on saying and doing what you are convinced is right. I have written my corre-spondents and satisfied them that they have no need to be anxious.'

Generosity like this, it hardly needs to be said, rarely failed to win an answering loyalty. It awoke in men powers whose very existence they themselves had scarce suspected. It was a daily challenge to them to do and to give of their best. ' I always felt,' one man writes, ' he saw and ex-pected something bigger in myself than I ever dreamed could be possible.' ' His extraordinary faith in us,' says another, ' we felt we simply had to justify.' ' I would have done anything,' says yet another, ' rather than let him down.' Nowhere are we nearer the secret of the success of the Man-chester Mission than in simple, heartfelt words like these. When through all ranks of his army a general can kindle and spread so great a fire of devotion, he has already more than half won his battle.

# CHAPTER VII

## THE PREACHER

THIS book is throughout the story of a preacher's life and work; but this chapter on Collier ' the Preacher ' will not be a long one. Some may even think that, short as it is, it might have been omitted altogether. ' Collier is no preacher,' men used to say, who had none but the kindliest feelings about him or his work; and it was quite commonly assumed that whatever it was that brought the crowds to the services of the Mission, it was certainly not the preaching. And, of course, nobody would claim that Collier was in any sense what is called a ' great ' preacher. Representatives of the Press—even of the religious Press—though they often sought him out to learn about the social work of the Mission, did not go to find ' good copy ' in his sermons. His preaching was indeed often commonplace in matter, and, as one of his best friends once said, ' appallingly casual ' in manner. How could it be otherwise when we remember how little time his crowded days and nights left him for pulpit preparation? He told his friend Gipsy Smith that on one occasion it was four o'clock on Sunday afternoon before he got his first chance to look at his text for his evening sermon

in the Free Trade Hall; and, he said, ' when I
sat down at my desk I felt so absolutely worn out
that before I knew what I was doing I was asleep,
and I slept soundly till five o'clock. But I had
my sermon.' ' Of course you had,' said the Gipsy,
' the Lord would rather let the sky fall than not
give you a sermon after such a week's work.'

Nevertheless, the fact remains that on nearly
every Sunday for twenty-one years Collier preached
in the Free Trade Hall to the largest Methodist
congregation in the world. One recalls Abraham
Lincoln's famous saying, that you may fool all the
people some of the time, and some of the people
all the time, but you can't fool all the people all
the time. And when, not merely for the few short
weeks of a ' Special Mission,' but year after year,
through a whole generation, a man gathers and
holds crowds such as those that regularly waited
on Collier's ministry, it simply will not do to say
that he was ' no preacher.' His successor, the
Rev. Herbert Cooper, who took up the burden
when it fell from his dead chief's shoulders, says
that what amazes him most as he looks back is
the way in which all through the strenuous years
he managed to find week by week a word in season
for his great congregation. What was the secret
of his power ?

Much and very much is, undoubtedly, to be
attributed to causes which lay outside the sermon
itself. The great Free Trade Hall is always a
popular meeting-place with Manchester folk. Hymn

sheets were provided, and of course all sittings were free and unappropriated. The type of service, too—reverent but never stiff and formal, with a certain unbuttoned ease and infectious gladness about it—appealed to multitudes who found little to attract them in the ordinary routine of the Church's worship. And in addition to all this, Collier, like the wise general that he always was, had his trusty scouts posted at strategic points all over the great building, whose business it was to look out for the stranger, to make him feel that he was not only welcome but wanted, and in a hundred ways to seek to create the atmosphere in which it is easy alike to speak and to hear. But things like these, though they may explain much, do not explain everything; they may tell us why the crowd came, they do not tell why it kept on coming; nor is there any explanation short of the power of the preacher himself. Yet when we try to analyse and define that power we do not get very far. Collier published no sermons, and he has left, so far as can be discovered, only five in manuscript, all of them written during his early years and long before the beginning of his work in Manchester. One of them, which exists in duplicate, is the sermon which he preached as a student at the usual week evening service in the College Chapel, Didsbury. I turned to it with no little interest to find in it, if I could, some hint of his coming power; but quite in vain. It is just such a sermon as is written every year by hundreds of young preachers : very orthodox, very decorous, and, it must be added, very dull. There are no quotations except from the Bible, and no illustrations to relieve the general greyness. The subject is ' Spiritual Relationship to Christ,' and the text, *Whosoever shall do the will of My Father which is in heaven, the same is My brother and sister and mother.* The divisions of the sermon—Spiritual Relationship : (1) What it is not ; (2) What it is— show the influence of a safe and familiar model, but it is easy to see that the preacher has not yet found himself ; the voice is only an echo ; it is saying the correct rather than the vital thing. The living presence of the speaker may have been able to blow the ashes into a flame, but the last glint of fire has faded from them now. I am at the further disadvantage in writing of Collier as a preacher that, though I heard him speak on many different occasions, I never heard him preach. In what follows, therefore, I am compelled to lean on my general knowledge of the man himself, and on what I have been able to learn from others. If it does not satisfy those who owe him their own souls, it will at least, I hope, do him no injustice.

On one point, happily, it is possible to speak with emphasis. Collier's popularity as a preacher owed nothing to a vulgar and strident sensationalism. As these pages show, he broke fearlessly with many ancient conventions for the sake of the suffering souls and bodies of men ; but his daring was always well in hand, always obedient to a certain sober self-restraint which never forsook him and was, indeed, one of his most marked characteristics. And nowhere did this show itself more clearly than in his arrangement and conduct of the Sunday services of the Mission. Nor was he really as ' casual ' in his pulpit work as he often appeared. With no time for scholarship himself, he was always ready to make use of what the scholar could put at his service. ' If,' he said to a colleague once, ' I can hammer out a text in the Greek and get at its general meaning, I am satisfied now, and plunge into the subject I want to get at.' Nor was it only scholars whom he laid under contribution. He foraged in many fields and rarely returned home empty-handed. Pencil and pad were always at hand to jot down incidents, quotations, anecdotes—anything with which he might feather his arrow when Sunday came round.

One of the first elements of Collier's success as a preacher was the relation in which he and his huge congregation stood to each other. He had a genius for establishing at once easy and intimate relations with men, and he carried it with him into the pulpit. The crowd and he were together straightway—' in touch,' as they say in the army. Thy soul was like a star, and dwelt apart '—there was none of that feeling towards him. People remembered the open door at the Central Hall—that door without a latch, which swung easily on its own hinges—and it seemed to them an emblem of the man who was their minister. There were no great airs about him which frightened them : he was homely, accessible, a fellow-traveller ' on life's common way.' They remembered, too, multitudes of them, how much they owed him, what duties for their sakes he had laid upon his heart, with what ceaseless toil he had spent himself for them and for theirs. And when he preached, that was the background from which he spoke; that was the sounding board which flung out even his most halting and commonplace words. Was it any wonder that they heard him gladly? 'His word thunders whose life lightens.' But the casual visitor—the man who sometimes went away saying, 'Collier's no preacher'—easily missed all this. For him the background and the sounding board were not there. He might know in a general kind of way something of what was going on, but it did not mean to him what it meant to the men and women in Collier's congregation. For a similar reason Collier was often comparatively ineffective and disappointing when he preached away from home. He needed his own people to bring out the best that was in him. And to their and his credit alike be it said, for the most part they preferred him to the 'star' preachers who occasionally took his place. 'Yes, very good,' they would say when the great man had gone his way, 'but we 'd rather have our own man.' 'Give me Mr. Collier; we understand him.'

There were certain obvious qualities in Collier's preaching which it may be well to set down in a paragraph or two. They were all of the serviceable rather than of the showy order; they did not dazzle, they warmed ; and what is most important in a long ministry like his, they wore well. Mr. Frank T. Bullen, the well-known writer of sea stories, wrote after attending an evening service in the Free Trade Hall : ' I heard a plain, simple Gospel address on the text, *No man careth for my soul.* None of the arts of the practised orator were employed, none of that flamboyant extravagance of language which make some popular preachers such a draw, and in the eyes of Christian folk such a failure, but the homely, straight, sensible talk, such as C. H. Spurgeon used to favour us with in old Tabernacle days. And, listening to him, I could understand how such quiet, reasonable exhortation had still the power, despite modern dicta upon the foolishness of preaching, to fill this great place with eager listeners all the year round.' ' Mr. Collier,' said another visitor—' H. K.' of the *Methodist Recorder* (the late Nehemiah Curnock) —' has a good presence, a kindly face, a clear, resounding voice, and no mannerisms. The universal testimony is that his preaching is always fresh and practical, and there is in it a trumpet note of hope and joy.'

Homely, straight, sensible, practical—these are all right adjectives by which to describe Collier's preaching. His speech was

> ' rife
> With rugged maxims hewn from life.'

Sayings, incidents, anecdotes he made use of freely ; but he never went far to seek them ; he chose by preference those of a homely, familiar type. He took the common stones that lie about at all men's feet, and built with them ; to adorn what he built he had neither wit nor will. If he could make his meaning clear and get his point home, that was all he sought and all he cared for. Clean and sparkling water in a common tumbler—such was Collier's preaching. Nor was the water less refreshing for the homely vessel that held it. On the contrary, the preaching told by its sagacity and simplicity, by the way in which it came ' home to men's business and bosoms.' A member of his congregation has told me with what impressiveness she once heard him urge upon foremen their responsibility for keeping clean and wholesome the speech and atmosphere of their workshops, for the sake of the boys and girls who were coming into them straight from home and school. ' The most common-sense preacher I ever heard ' was the verdict of an old Scottish tutor who resided in Manchester and who sometimes found his way to the services of the Mission.

But once more, all this, true as it is, leaves much still untold. There must have been something in the preacher beyond these obvious, homespun qualities to draw and hold the multitudes through so many years. As I have said before, Collier was always and in everything the evangelist; but a certain spaciousness of outlook—his natural ' healthy-mindedness,' as William James might have called it—saved him from the intellectual

' Holding faith and a good conscience ; which some having thrust from them made shipwreck concerning the faith.'—(1 Tim. i. 19.)

Passion Week—Lantern Service.

' Go quickly, and tell His disciples, He is risen from the dead ; and lo, He goeth before you into Galilee ; there shall ye see Him.'—(Matt. xxviii. 7.)

' There cometh to Him a leper, beseeching Him, and kneeling down to Him, and saying unto Him, If Thou wilt, Thou canst make me clean.'—(Mark i. 40.)

' In all these things we are more than conquerors through Him that loved us.'—(Rom. viii. 37.)

' It is expedient for you that I go away : for if I go not away, the Comforter will not come unto you; but if I go, I will send Him unto you. And He, when He is come, will convict the world in respect of sin, and of righteousness, and of judgment.'—(John xvi. 7, 8.)

I must not conclude these brief notes on Collier the Preacher without some reference to an incident which occurred at the very outset of his ministry, to which he himself referred in public again and again, and which left undoubtedly a very deep and abiding impression upon his whole life. It is best stated, perhaps, in a paragraph which appeared in the *Methodist Recorder* during his year of office as President of the Conference. The paragraph, which was written with Collier's knowledge and approval by one of his younger colleagues, is as follows :—

' Those who have the privilege of attending

Mr. Collier's services during his great tour will discover that, in almost every one of them, at least one of the hymns selected will have reference to the Holy Spirit. For many years this has been Mr. Collier's custom, and he was led to adopt it as the result of an incident which he regards as one of the most significant and influential in his life. On the first Sunday he spent in a circuit, after leaving College, a crowded congregation faced him in the evening, and many remained to the after-meeting. But the atmosphere was hard, and there seemed to be no response to his appeal. Just at that juncture Mrs. Brown, the wife of Mr. Collier's superintendent, came and whispered into his ear : "Mr. Collier, do you think we are sufficiently honouring the Holy Ghost ? " The young preacher told the congregation of the question put to him, and he added : "We have not had a hymn referring to the Spirit to-night, nor has any one mentioned Him in prayer. Let us spend a few moments in silent meditation on that theme." They did so, and a hymn to the Spirit was sung. Almost immediately a mighty wave of power swept the meeting ; and there were many wonderful conversions. Mr. Collier regards the experience as a lesson and a rebuke.' [1]

The writer, in sending the paragraph to me, adds : ' It raises difficulties for me ; and I believe Mr. Collier felt these also. But he regarded it as one of the most vital experiences that ever came to him, and he acted upon it.' Many others, probably,

[1] If the details are correctly given the incident must have occurred in the Brentford Circuit, and therefore at the beginning of Collier's second year in the ministry. (See chap. ii.)

will be conscious of the ' difficulties ' of which my correspondent speaks. We read in the New Testament : *The Father hath given all judgment unto the Son ; that all may honour the Son, even as they honour the Father. He that honoureth not the Son honoureth not the Father which sent Him.* But the New Testament writers nowhere speak of honouring the Holy Spirit ; it is doubtful indeed if they would have understood what was meant by it. Surely the Spirit is honoured wherever and whenever Christ is honoured, and to speak of ' honouring the Holy Spirit ' as of something distinct from honouring Christ is to come perilously near the edge of un-reality ; it is to make a distinction which has neither intellectual validity nor religious value. But whatever Collier was, he was not unreal ; behind his language, however we may criticise it, there lay a really vital experience—his sense of the Divine presence and power in his ministry and with his word. And when he spoke of ' honouring the Holy Spirit,' it was but his way of witnessing to it ; it was his equivalent of the prophetic conscious-ness in the strength of which men dared to say of words which were still their own : *Thus saith the Lord.*

When Moody—a man whom Collier in many ways resembled—paid his first visit to Birmingham, Dale was one of those who were equally impressed and perplexed by his evident power. ' At the first meeting,' he wrote, ' Mr. Moody's address was simple, direct, kindly, and hopeful ; it had a

touch of humour and a touch of pathos ; it was lit
up with a story or two that filled most eyes with
tears ; but there was nothing in it very remarkable.
Yet it *told.* . . . At the evening meeting the same
day, at Bingley Hall, I was still unable to make out
how it was that he had done so much in other parts
of the kingdom.   I listened with interest ; everybody listened with interest ; and I was conscious
again of a certain warmth and brightness which
made the service very pleasant, but I could not see
that there was much to impress those that were
careless about religious duty.   The next morning
at the prayer meeting the address was more incisive
and striking, and at the evening service I began to
see that the stranger had a faculty for making the
elementary truths of the Gospel intensely clear and
vivid.   But it still seemed most remarkable that
he should have done so much, and I told Mr. Moody
that the work was most plainly of God, for I could
see no real relation between him and what he had
done.   He laughed cheerily, and said he should be
very sorry if it were otherwise.'   With scarcely a
change the whole passage might stand—and this
is my apology for quoting it—as a pen-portrait of
Collier.   The warmth and brightness of the service ;
the simplicity, directness, and hopefulness of the
speaker ;   the   touch   of   humour,   the   frequent
anecdote ;   the   obvious   interest   of   the   crowd—it
is all here as there, down to the inevitable ' there
was nothing in it very remarkable,' and the repeated  wonder that such  ordinary means  should

achieve such extraordinary results. Nor does the parallel fail us when we come to the end of the passage : it was all ' most plainly of God.' And in saying that we are telling everything, and we are telling nothing, of the secret of Collier's power as a preacher.

# CHAPTER VIII

## THE PHILANTHROPIST

> ' Unto the poor
> Among mankind he was in service bound,
> As by some tie invisible, oaths professed
> To a religious order.'
>
> (*The Prelude*, Book ix.).

IF one were to ask any chance half-dozen members of the religious public of Manchester for what the Manchester Mission stands, the very variety of the answers he would probably receive would be in itself a witness to the many-sidedness of the Mission's activities. To one it suggests the sight of a vast festive throng which, at the November Anniversary, crowds the Free Trade Hall three times in one day. For this the Methodist tribes come up every year from all the region round about; and for some this is their sole point of contact with the Mission or its work. For others the chief point of interest is the Tuesday mid-day service which, except for a few weeks in the height of summer, has been carried on without a break through all the years of the Mission's history. To others again—and when we remember that the Mission has in its Sunday schools some 6000 scholars and teachers, and 5000 on its roll of church membership, the number of these must be very large—the Mission is their religious ' home.' For many of them life is bleak and lonely, and the Mission—perhaps in the person of a kindly ' Sister ' —is their one living link with the world of sympathy and fellowship and service. Men and women who have their own comfortable homes, and troops of generous friends always about them, may not appreciate what this means ; but those who know from experience how lonely a place a great city can be will not need to be told. And then, over and above all such, there are those who have lost even such slender footing as they had on the lower rungs of the social ladder, but who in the Homes or Refuges of the Mission have received not only ' charity,' but that touch of human kindness for which ignominy always thirsts. It is of Collier's work for these last—the men and women who are the shame and the menace of our Christian civilisation—that something will be said in this chapter.

In that noble poem, some lines of which are quoted above, Wordsworth tells us how, in the early days of the French Revolution, he and his friend Michel Beaupuy

> ' chanced
> One day to meet a hunger-bitten girl,
> Who crept along fitting her languid gait
> Unto a heifer's motion, by a cord
> Tied to her arm, and picking thus from the lane
> Its sustenance, while the girl with pallid hands
> Was busy knitting in a heartless mood
> Of solitude, and at the sight my friend
> In agitation said, " 'Tis against *that*
> That we are fighting." '

And it was against *that*, in the manifold shapes that it can assume in the life of a huge, modern industrial city, that Collier fought—nor did his sword sleep in his hand—for more than thirty years. Step by step he felt his way until he had thought out and put together as complete a bit of social machinery as could, perhaps, be found anywhere in Christendom. ' Collier,' said an enthusiastic writer in the *Daily Chronicle*, ' is a Universal Brotherhood Provider,' and his Mission ' a Harrod's Stores of religious and social activities ' ; ' there is nothing in the way of fraternity you cannot procure at his depôt, from a clean bed to a new life.' How came a young Methodist preacher to make work of this sort ' church ' work ? to embark on an adventure which, thirty years ago, was as novel and daring as it was difficult ?

At the outset it should be clearly understood that work of the kind represented, say, by the Labour Yard and the Maternity Home, was in no sense the carrying out of an elaborate programme which some clever draughtsman had prepared in advance. Collier's mind was essentially of the soberly practical order ; he dreamed his dreams and saw his visions, but his feet were never off the solid earth. Startling as some of his methods may have seemed to the worshippers of the great goddess ' Ydgrun '—as Samuel Butler calls her—there was really nothing in him of the revolutionary. On some points, indeed, which have long since passed out of the region of debate—such, for example, as the employment of a paid ' Sisterhood '—he had at first very grave misgivings; and though he fought his way through them, he remained to the end by instinct a conservative. There is, perhaps, no better proof of this than what happened just before the Central Hall was opened in 1886. The young missioner was asked for his programme. The most novel items in it were these: free seats for all, a free hand in advertising, a popular Sunday afternoon service, a Saturday night concert, and a brass band—nothing very terrifying there, one would have thought, even to the ' Ydgrunites ' themselves. The social work of the Mission, it will be noticed, which afterwards became so conspicuous, is here conspicuous only by its absence. The truth is, Collier took up the social work simply because he could not help himself, and almost in spite of himself. He was, as I have said, essentially conservative in temperament, just as Wesley was; but, happily, as in Wesley, so in him, the practical Dr. Jekyll could at any time get the better of the theorising Mr. Hyde. If this and that were necessary in order to the salvation of men, then this and that must be done, whatever Mesdames Use and Wont might think or say. I repeat, it was no pre-determined theory about the relation of the Church to our modern social problems which led Collier to open a Men's Refuge and a Women's Shelter; these things were forced on him in order that he might do the work of an evangelist. A few words will make this clear.

What first opened Collier's eyes to the nature
and magnitude of the problem confronting him
was those midnight walks round Lever Street,
during his early days in Manchester, to which I
have already referred.[1] Like another Nehemiah,
before calling on others to rise up and build, he
arose by night and saw for himself the evil case
of Jerusalem, how her walls were broken down,
and her gates burned with fire, until his heart
was seared by the shame and reproach of it all.
Then came the opening of the Central Hall, and
the immediate success of the work there, which
lit up for him, as by a lightning flash, vast ruined
areas of the city's life with which he had no means
to cope. The miserable, the unfortunate, the
ne'er-do-weel found their way in increasing numbers
to the services of the Mission ; and these were the
very people it had been established to reach and
to save ; but its success was its perplexity : what
could it do for them now that it had got them ?
how could it save them now that it had reached
them ?  The marches of the Mission bands through
the streets, at midnight on Saturday, and again
on Sunday afternoons, brought in in their train
squads of starving and homeless men, for whom
something must be done and done at once. Men
who had read the New Testament could not be
guilty of the hypocrisy of offering hymn books to
the hungry ; their bodily needs must somehow be
met, if services and sermons were to have any

[1] See p. 42.

chance with them. But this was only the thin end of the difficulty. Collier insisted that, in order to do its proper work, the Central Hall doors must be open not only on Sundays and in the evenings, but every day and all day long ; [1] and this meant before long an unending and strangely mingled stream of applicants : the professional ' cadger,' of course, but besides him men and women who were silly rather than wicked ; casual labourers, honest but feckless, and the first to suffer when the pinch of bad times comes ; ticket-of-leave men, whom nobody will employ ; hard-working women with little children and a sick husband ; young girls in trouble—forlorn suitors all of them in Pity's wide court.

What then was to be done ? It was no use for the young preacher to say, ' Conference sent me not to feed the hungry, but to preach the Gospel, and to save the souls of men ' ; how should a man care about either his ' soul ' or its ' salvation ' who had nothing to eat and nowhere to sleep ? Collier had deliberately elected to make the Central Hall a place where the worst might be sure of a welcome ; he had taken as his motto, ' The utmost for the lowest ' ; he had, therefore, either to deny the first article of his creed as a missioner, or face the consequences, whatever they might be. Of course he faced them, and the social work of the Mission

---

[1] The doors, Collier noted with satisfaction, were swing doors, like the doors of the public-house. No publican, he said, put handles on his doors—the customers would not always be able to find them if he did '—and the doors of the Central Hall must be as easy to open.

began. The first steps, naturally, were of the simplest kind. Hungry men who followed the crowd into the popular Sunday afternoon service were given food and drink.[1] Homeless men were supplied with a ticket of admission into one of the city lodging-houses. To meet the case of those who were willing to work but who could get no work to do, Collier had resort to all manner of odd devices. One man he 'set up' as a hawker of dripping; for another, an ex-schoolmaster, he hired a wheelbarrow, and stocked it with sweets. He had gone into business, he used to tell his friends, and was now senior partner in the firm of ' Collier and ——, Lozenge Merchants.' It is good to know that the 'firm' prospered at least to this extent, that it helped the junior partner back to his teaching again. But all this, as Collier quickly came to see, was but nibbling at the fringe of his problem. Gradually it was forced upon him that just where the need was direst, his old methods were useless, and would continue to be useless until they were supplemented by others of a new and different type. Already the attempt to provide for the homeless in the lodging-houses of the city was breaking down

[1] One of Collier's many good stories has to do with this simple Sunday afternoon meal. A rough-looking man turned up at his office one morning: 'I've come to bring you a bob, sir,' he said. 'Well,' said Collier, 'I've no objection to receiving bobs, but I like to know what they are for.' 'Why, it's this way,' said the man, 'I've been here two Sundays and got a good feed each time as put new heart into me. I'd never had to beg before, but things had been cruel hard and I was hungry. Now I've got some work, and thinks I, I'm going to give a bob out of it to help some other poor chap that's in the same hole as I was.'

in his hands. What the men who drifted into the Central Hall most needed—oversight, restraint, sympathy—the common lodging-house could do nothing to supply. There was only one thing for it—the Mission must have a ' Home ' of its own. Again the beginning was of the humblest kind. An old, disused rag factory in Hood Street, Ancoats, was cleared and cleaned and opened, in March 1891, as a Men's Home and Shelter.

From this time forward, the social work of the Mission—to make a distinction which, in Collier's mind at least, was never more than verbal—went on side by side with the evangelistic. For some years it was sadly hampered by want of means of every kind ; and indeed, as yet, Collier himself hardly knew what he wanted. The work was new, and the worker himself had everything to learn. Only by experiment and failure could he find out the kind of equipment which was best fitted for his purpose. Ten years later he had learned his lesson ; a generous public which had watched and approved was ready with the money ; and in 1901, amid the benedictions of the city fathers, and the goodwill of all good citizens, a new Home was erected on the site (enlarged) of the old, which has again and again been described as one of the most admirably planned and completely equipped of its kind in the country.

If I were writing a report and not a biography, this would be the place at which to give some account both of the building itself and of the work which now for more than twenty years has been carried on in it.   As it is I shall mention only one fact, and that for the light which it throws on the sanity of Collier's methods in the field of social reform.   Like all other workers in that field, he had had painful experience of the way in which the State has succeeded in making its ' charity ' utterly hateful in the eyes of those who are sometimes driven to accept it.   For example, if a man sought the shelter of one of the State's Casual Wards, he got his supper, a board to lie on, and a breakfast. Then, in the morning, he had to pay for his entertainment by spending the only hours of the day in which there is the least hope of finding work in picking oakum or breaking stones.   Collier's plan was the reverse of this.   Men were taken into the Home in the early afternoon, and set to work chopping wood and making up bundles by which they earned supper, bed and breakfast.   As Collier said, that paid him because he got the work before he gave the meal ;  and it paid the man, because then he was free to start early in the morning on his search for a job.   If he succeeded, well and good ; if not, he could return again in the afternoon and earn another night's lodgings.

Work of this kind, done on such common-sense principles, and on the scale which the new premises now made possible, were certain soon to attract attention, and in 1902 circumstances combined to give it something like a national advertisement. During the winter of that year, as a result of some proceedings in the local police court, the Manchester public was startled and shocked to discover that hundreds of homeless men were sleeping out every night in the brick-crofts near to the city, while the Casual Ward maintained by the ratepayers was three-fourths empty. For nine days the ' Sleeping-out Scandal ' was the talk of the town, and the searchlight of the investigator was turned, not only on the ways of Poor Law Guardians, but on the various philanthropic organisations of the city. Collier and his helpers could have asked for nothing better, and the result was a triumphant vindication of their methods. The writer of an article on ' The Vagrancy Problem,' which appeared in the *Manchester Guardian*, singled out the Hood Street Home as ' a model of efficiency.' A special committee appointed by the City Council to inspect the Homes and Shelters of the city paid a surprise visit at midnight, and had nothing but commendation for all they saw and heard ; ' the Mission,' they said, ' was teaching the Poor Law experts how to deal with the vagrant.' And, finally, the Local Government Inspector reported that in his judgment ' both the building and the system adopted seem admirably calculated to attain the objects the Mission has in view, while the admirable order in which the whole place is kept is worthy of all praise.' [1]

For the reason already given—that this book is

[1] I am indebted for the facts of this paragraph to the admirable Report, written in 1903, by the Rev. H. M. Nield, who was for six years one of Collier's colleagues.

the story of a man, not of a movement—I must pass over with a bare word of mention the many other social agencies which, as the years went by, sprang up one by one to meet some newly-discovered need. The following slightly abridged summary, which I take from the twenty-seventh Annual Report, will give an outline which the reader may fill in for himself :—

'The social work of the Mission has been carried on during the year with unabated vigour and with marked success. The need for such effort was never more apparent. The centres for rescue, relief, and preventive work are well built and conveniently situated. The head offices are at the Central Buildings, Oldham Street. This section of the Mission is entirely unsectarian. It is estimated that over 41,500 persons in search of advice and help have availed themselves of the " open door " of the Mission during the past twelve months. The Homes and Refuges have accommodation for 450. Sunday meals for the destitute were provided last year for 27,560 men. The Maternity Home and Hospital has cared for a large number of young mothers. The employment bureaux during the year have provided permanent and temporary posts for workless men and women. By means of the Fresh Air Fund worn-out women and girls, and crippled and sick children were enabled to have rest and change during the summer months. Work amongst discharged prisoners has been carried on with growing success. Rescue work in the streets, by midnight missions, visits to public-houses late at night, and other special efforts, has also been undertaken with marked results.

' Amongst the auxiliary agencies of the Mission must be mentioned the Cripples' Guild, with fortnightly " Parlours," weekly industrial classes and holiday arrangements. The homes of the cripples are visited regularly by a nurse, and by lady visitors. Workhouses, hospitals, cab-stands, etc., are regularly visited by Mission workers. The Sunshine Brigade, Dorcas Society, Benevolent Society, and similar agencies are worked by volunteers, and care specially for the lonely, the sick, and the poor.'

There was one item in the week's work, which is not included in the foregoing summary, but which had its place in Collier's programme from the first, and to which he attached the utmost importance : I mean the Saturday night concert. I give a paragraph to it here because, commonplace as the story is now, it is throughout so typical of the man and his methods. Let it be understood, then, that the Saturday night meeting was not a religious service in disguise ; it was what it was called, a Popular Concert. Its aim was to provide music and amusement for the million ; it was the Mission's contribution to the Saturday night pro-blem of our great cities. ' Saturday night,' Collier used to say, ' is the devil's busiest night.' But what, he asked himself, is the good of declaiming against the public-house, or the disreputable music hall, if you do nothing else ? What were the people to do ? Where were they to go ? And so he determined that, if they would, they should come to the Central Hall. A weekly programme was arranged of first-rate quality ; he would have no ambitious amateurs eager for a chance to ' try their voices ' ; he engaged competent artistes and paid them their fees.[1] One penny—later raised to twopence—was the charge for admission. Even those who cannot sit through a concert without something to eat and drink were not forgotten ; they got their chance in the interval. Of course —this was nearly forty years ago, be it remembered —there was a loud clamour among the ' Ydgrunites.' How, they asked, could you expect to do any good on Sunday in a hall in which a woman in a low-necked dress sang a secular song the night before ? But Collier was not to be moved ; he had counted the cost, and he held on his way. He was always in charge of the concert himself, and he would allow nothing in the programme that was vulgar or unseemly ; [2] but he could not believe that he was imperilling any sacred interest committed to him as a minister when he tried to weave this tiny thread of colour into the drab and cheerless lives of the multitudes around him. ' I count that day basely spent,' Lord Morley once said, ' in

[1] In those early years the well-known singers, Madame Kirkby Lunn and Madame Sadler Fogg, both used to sing at these concerts.

[2] For example, writing to Mrs. Collier, who was away from home, he says (Oct. 15, 1907): ' Last night we had a good concert; a great pack. In the cinematograph entertainment a film came on that I did not like, so I stopped it at once. All went on smoothly afterwards. There was nothing *very* objectionable, but I thought it rather vulgar, and not our sort. I spoke to the people about the difficulty of keeping entertainments pure and good. I think the whole thing would be beneficial. The people applauded my action. It would make the young people think.'

which no thought is given to the life of the garret and the hovel.' It was always of these that Collier was thinking, and never more sincerely than when he planned his Popular Saturday Evening Concerts.

It will, perhaps, be said by some that work of the kind referred to in this chapter is work that ought not to be left to private and individual enterprise; that it should be made the responsibility of the State; and that, in any case, it is no part of the work of the Church. These are not questions that can be discussed here, but I may indicate what would probably have been Collier's answer. In the first place, he would have said that whether it was the work of the State or not, in point of fact the State was not doing it. In 1901, the year in which the Men's Home was opened, there were neither old-age pensions, nor out-of-work doles, to soften the hard lot of the helpless poor. And if some one had urged that it was the duty of those who cared for the poor not to concern themselves with mere palliatives, but to work for reforms that would remove the disease itself, Collier might have answered, ' Yes, work for them by all means; but meanwhile, here is John Jones, hungry, homeless, helpless—what is to be done with him ? ' And, still further, I think he would have said that when the State has done all that it can do, there will still be room and need for work like this; for the ways of the State are hard, and redemption comes only through love, and the service which love inspires. As for those who said that work of this kind was no part of the work of the Church, Collier's position was simply this : not once nor twice but many times, from the beginning and all along, he had set forth as the great aim and hope of the Mission the redemption of the most hopeless. The faith of his favourite text—*Able to save to the uttermost*—was the chief corner-stone of all its activities. ' A Mission of this class,' he wrote in one of his annual Reports, ' attracts the cadger, the lazy loafer, the half-imbecile victim of hereditary pauperism. It frankly wishes to do so. It would fain lay its hand on the wrecks of humanity, touching the leper and raising the paralytic. They are the despair of magistrates and poor law guardians. They prey upon society, and add ceaselessly to the difficulties of social reformers and statesmen. Here is hopelessness in the concrete. The Mission never shrinks from the tasks of dealing with it.' And would any deny that work like this was the work of the Church ? But, as Collier soon discovered, it was work which, with only such tools as lay ready to his hand, could never be done. Either, then, he must be content to leave the ' poor devils ' of the street to the Salvation Army, or to the tender mercies of the Casual Ward, or *he must find some way of lengthening the reach of his arm.* That, in a single word, is the whole philosophy of the social work of the Manchester Mission.

One question still remains : did this work in Collier's hands become merely an end in itself ? or, was there through it all a Divine upthrust ? Did it prove in any real sense redemptive ?  What is known as the ' Institutional Church ' has become during recent years a very familiar feature of English religious life ;  but, while one is thankful for any evidence of honest concern on the part of the Church for her unfulfilled duty to the world, he may yet doubt both the wisdom and the worth of a good deal that goes on under the shelter of that elastic phrase.  In matters of this sort it is not so much what we think good that counts as what we put first ;  it is a question of emphasis, and so often, alas, the emphasis comes on the wrong thing.  In the most widely read novel of recent years—Mr. A. S. M. Hutchinson's *If Winter Comes*—the author says :—

> ' Man cannot live by bread alone, the Churches tell him ;  but he says, " I *am* living on bread alone, and doing well on it."  But I tell you, Hapgood, that plump down in the crypt and abyss of every man's soul is a hunger, a craving for other food than this earthy stuff.  And the Churches know it ;  and instead of reaching down to him what he wants—light, light— instead of that they invite him to dancing and picture shows, and you 're a jolly good fellow, and religion 's a jolly fine thing and no spoil- sport, and all that sort of latter-day tendency. Why, man, he can get all that outside the Churches and get it better.  Light, light !  He wants light, Hapgood.  And the padres come

down and drink beer with him and dance jazz with him, and call it making religion a Living Thing in the Lives of the People. Lift the hearts of the people to God, they say, by showing them that religion is not incompatible with having a jolly fine time. *And there's no God there that a man can understand for him to be lifted up to.*'

I do not think that any fair critic ever brought a charge like that against the Manchester Mission. Writing in the early days of the Great War, Collier said, ' In all its manifold activities the Mission continues to prosecute its main purpose, the salvation of the individual through the preaching of Jesus Christ. Every agency is judged by this test.' And, happily, there is tangible and abundant evidence that the purpose was realised. A few illustrations have already been given on an earlier page.[1] But the most striking evidence was furnished by Collier himself in 1907, when he appeared as a witness before a Royal Commission on the Poor Laws and the Relief of Distress. He was asked if he could give the names of men and women who had been rescued from drink and other evil habits, and were now sober and respectable citizens. ' Certainly,' said Collier, ' you shall have as many as you like ' ; and in three days a list of over a hundred names—fifty-three men and fifty women —was prepared and forwarded. It lies before me as I write, and I select four entries from each section. There is nothing whatever exceptional

[1] See p. 79.

about those I have chosen, and the complete list, it must be remembered, is itself but an extract from the carefully kept records of the Mission :—

'F. H.—Came to us from prison. He had been an hotel clerk, but through drinking habits he had got wrong. He made a great effort to reform, and at last a situation was found for him in his own particular line which he has retained. Three years' record.

'W. H.—Came to us with a bad character from Warwick gaol. He had suffered twelve terms of imprisonment. He has proved worthy of help, and has worked nobly and well for four years. Four years' record.

'J. S.—Sold up his home again and again, disgraced his children after his wife's death, and finally forsook them. He was hiding in Manchester. An anonymous letter came to us and we found him. From the time of his entrance into our Home he gave up the drink, and became a thoughtful, God-fearing man. He now keeps in touch with his children, and in every way lives a consistent life.

'G. R.—Was out of work, destitute and friendless. After months of waiting and working as a casual we recommended him as storekeeper. He secured the situation, and by industry gained the good opinion of all. He married, and is now a good citizen. Fifteen years' record.

'M. K.—An orphan, has two sisters, but they would do nothing for her. When nineteen gave birth to a child in the workhouse ; it died while she was there. Came to us quite destitute. We kept her for a time, and then found her a situation which she retained for three years. She is now an assistant in a coffee tavern. Good record.

'A. J.—Age 49. Came from one of the Unions in North Wales. Entered the Refuge, July 1897. Remained with us a few months, was sent to a situation as children's nurse, and is still in the same family, doing well. She had been in the habit of giving way to drink, but has not touched it for the last nine years. Nine years' record.

'C. H.—Age 24. Slept in the Casual Ward the night before she came to our Refuge, October 1897. She was an orphan and quite destitute. We kept her for five months, and then found her a situation a few miles out of Manchester. She remained in the same family a number of years, and the last time she called told us of her approaching marriage. Her mistress gave her an excellent character. Nine years' record.

'L. T.—Age 15. Her mother had been in the Refuge in 1900. Drink had made the mother a complete wreck, and she begged that we would save her daughter from the same fate. L. was one of five illegitimate children, and had never known what it was to have proper food or a decent home. We cared for and then sent her to a friend of the Mission to be trained in household duties. She remained for nearly four years, and then left to take a better situation. She is now happily married to a steady young man. Seven years' record.'

It was, I think, a witty American who once said that Christians to-day are no longer content to play the part of the Good Samaritan to those who have fallen among robbers—they see to the policing of the Jericho road. The sentiment is entirely after Collier's own heart. As a rule he took no active part in the political or municipal life of his city ; but on two or three occasions, when some great moral issue was at stake, he intervened, and with striking effect.   Quite early in his Manchester days, for example, Alexander M'Laren and he went into the witness-box to protest against the granting of a drink licence to a place of popular amusement which had won for itself an evil reputation.   It was Collier's first fight of the kind, and both then and on a similar occasion in 1910, the protest was successful and the licence refused. He was greatly concerned for the purity of the administration of justice in the city, and more than once—it is hardly worth while recalling the circumstances now—he let it be known that there is a moral power in the community to which even Watch Committees and magistrates must be in subjection.   But it was not striving against sin in the field of public controversy that Collier's greatest triumphs were won.   He had none of the fiery eloquence, the fierce moral passion, the high crusading temper, which made men like his contemporaries, Hugh Price Hughes and Silvester Horne, so great a power in the public life of their time.   But, as this chapter has very imperfectly tried to show, he achieved success in a field where many faint and grow weary, and he left behind him an example of wise and patient well-doing in the cause of the neglected poor such as this generation has rarely seen.

# CHAPTER IX

## THE MAN

In every man's work there is always something of the man himself, and in the foregoing pages we have been watching Collier in his work at the same time that we have been watching him at it. Some few further touches, however, the picture still needs, if others are to see in it the man his friends knew and loved.

### I. SOME PERSONAL CHARACTERISTICS

Collier's character presented few problems to those who sought to read it. Forthrightness was the very nature of the man ; it showed itself in all he said and did and was. And with it there went the fearlessness which is so often the dower of simple hearts and which in him, as we have seen, sometimes bore the look of masterfulness ; men thought him impatient and brusque. And it is probably true that an organisation like the Manchester Mission could never have been created by a man cast in a gentler mould. Nevertheless, Collier usually had himself well in hand. ' If you lose your patience,' he used to say, ' you lose your influence.' One of his favourite texts was, *He that believeth shall not make haste.* ' He would be trying to dictate letters,' writes one of his clerical secretaries, ' when almost every sentence would be punctuated by a telephone call, or a knock on the door. Probably there would be a meeting to attend in a short time, and he would begin to feel " hustled." Suddenly he would pull up short, shake his head, smile quizzically and say, " He that believeth shall not make haste—eh, Miss H—— ? " ' Nor, with all his instinct and capacity for leadership, was he ever guilty of the meanness of thrusting down smaller men, and using them to exalt himself. Collier's colleagues always knew that they could count on him to give them their chance, and to find room and opportunity for any gifts that were theirs. To go through the Reports and other publications of the Mission during the thirty-six years of his superintendency, and to see how comparatively inconspicuous is the figure of the man who in the eyes of the public was ' the very pulse of the machine,' is to learn a lesson in true humility and self-effacement which will not soon be forgotten.

Perhaps nothing was more characteristic of Collier, or comes back more readily to his friends when they recall him, than his big, hearty, infectious laugh. He lived his daily life very near to ' the tears of things,' but nothing could kill the gaiety of his spirit. Few guessed how heavy were the burdens that he carried, he bore them with so light a heart ; his vigour was all ' radiant vigour ' ; sunshine and merriment went with him everywhere. ' The sad heart tires in a mile,' but joy in service is strength for service, and Collier held on his way because he refused to be depressed.

> ' Seasons impaired not the ray
> Of his buoyant cheerfulness clear.'

Indeed, good folk were sometimes taken aback by what seemed an almost dangerous leaning to levity in him. Casual acquaintances who met him at the Manchester Reform Club might say afterwards that he was ' a jolly good fellow,' but not exactly what you call a ' saint.' Well, of course, all depends upon what you mean by a ' saint.' If you mean the traditional saint of the Middle Ages, ' the saint that we see on the walls of every picture gallery in Europe, the saint that still haunts the imagination of hundreds of thousands of devout men who regard the Romish apostasy with horror—the thin, pale face, the eyes red with tears or weary with watching, the transparent hands, the wasted form ' : if that is our ideal of saintliness, then Collier was as little of a saint as Martin Luther himself.[1] Many

---

[1] The words quoted in the text are from Dale's striking chapter on ' Christian Worldliness.' What he says about Luther would serve very well as a portrait of Collier : ' His massive face and robust form were the outward and visible signs of the vigour and massiveness of his moral and religious character. He was a man, and did not try to be anything else : God made him a man, what was he that he should quarrel with God's work? He had flesh and blood ; he could not help it. He did not desire to help it. He ate heartily and enjoyed seeing his friends at dinner. He married a wife and loved her ; and he loved God none the less. He liked music and songs as well as psalms and sermons. He could laugh as well as preach. He had a genial humour as well as deep devoutness. He was a brave man, strong and resolute, with abounding life of all kinds ; a saint of a type with which, for many evil centuries, Christendom had been unfamiliar.'—*Laws of Christ for Common Life*, p. 235.

religious people, says ' Parson John ' in his letter
to ' Miriam Gray,' when they talk of religion have
a bedside manner, and walk about in felt slippers.
And if they speak of God, they always tidy themselves first.   But Collier was one of those who go
in and out of all the rooms in God's house as though
they were quite at home, who open the doors without knocking, and hum on the stairs, and it isn't
always hymns either.   ' He was splendidly human
to the very last fibre of him,' says his friend,
Dr. Campbell Morgan.  Good stories, animals,
games—he delighted in them all.  What an in-
exhaustible store of anecdotes he seemed to have,
and how he loved to share them with his friends,
both in public and in private !  Central Hall
memories, if not Central Hall records, could tell,
I fancy, of four-footed as well as human waifs and
strays that sometimes found a temporary refuge
there.   Among Collier's papers I came across an
old memorial card, with a black-edged border,
inscribed with mock solemnity in his own handwriting thus :—

' In
Loving Memory
of
Old Puss
who after 17 years' faithful service in
the same family was rewarded
by being drowned, Aug. 24, 1886.

"A joyful mother of children."
Ps. cxiii. 9.'

But to the last Collier had no keener interest,

outside his work and his home, than cricket. There is a picture of him bowling the first ball in a match at the opening of a sports' field which had been secured for the young people of the Mission. In a telegram to one of his sons who was on the Continent on his birthday, the one item of news added to the birthday greetings was : ' Yorkshire won 190.' And once, when he himself was on his way to Norway, and somebody on shipboard asked him about the Mission, he replied laughingly, ' I 'm not thinking much about the Mission now ; what I want to know is, is Lancashire going to beat Surrey ? '

It was homely, human qualities of this kind that helped to win for Collier that easy entrance at other men's doors which was so often noted in him. He had the happy knack of putting strangers at once and completely at their ease with him. He made friends with the guards on the tramcars, and the passengers, with whom he made his daily journeys to and from town. He would laugh and chat with them, ask them about their families, and by his frank and breezy ways would often put a brighter face on the morning of a dull day. ' While other men,' writes one who knew him in his college days, ' would wait and wonder if their overture would be understood and welcomed, Collier would get right home, brushing out of the way, with his cheery and genuine bonhomie, all mistrust and indifference.' It was always his way to ' walk right up and say " Hullo ! " ' Some well-known

American verses, of which this line is the refrain, adds the same correspondent, admirably describe Collier's manner, and for that reason I reproduce them in a footnote.[1] One little incident, trifling as it is, will serve to show that their simple philosophy of life was also his own : One day

[1] 'When you see a man in woe,
  Walk right up an' say " Hullo !"
  Say " Hullo !" and " How d' ye do ?"
  Slap the fellow on the back,
  Bring yer han' down with a whack ;
  Waltz right up an' don't go slow,
  Grin an' shake an' say " Hullo !"

  Is he clothed in rags ?  O sho !
  Walk right up an' say " Hullo !"
  Rags is but a cotton roll
  Jest for wrappin' up a soul ;
  An' a soul is worth a true
  Hale an' hearty " How d' ye do ?"
  Don't wait for the crowd to go ;
  Walk right up an' say " Hullo !"

  When large vessels meet, they say,
  They saloot an' sail away,
  Jest the same are you an' me
  Lonesome ships upon a sea ;
  Each one sailing his own jog
  For a port beyond the fog.
  Let yer speakin'-trumpet blow,
  Lift yer horn an' cry " Hullo !"

  Say " Hullo !" an' " How d' ye do ?'
  Other folk are good as you.
  When ye leave yer house of clay,
  Wanderin' in the Far-Away,
  When ye travel through the strange
  Country t' other side the range,
  Then the souls you 've cheered will know
  Who ye be, an' say " Hullo !" '

Miss Lena Ashwell, the famous actress, who used often to recite these lines to the men at the front during the War, says that this was always their favourite piece.

during the War he turned into a hairdresser's shop in Manchester for a shave. Many of the regular assistants were serving in the army, and a boy was employed to do the lathering. When he had finished his part of the operation, Collier said to him, ' Have you ever shaved anybody yet, my lad ? ' ' No, sir,' he answered. ' Then,' said Collier, ' have your first try on me.' ' Do you know who I am ? ' he added. ' Yes, sir,' said the boy, ' you 're Mr. Collier of the Central Hall.' ' Well, go ahead ! ' said Collier. The task was safely completed, and the lad went about the rest of the day's work with a glow of satisfaction at his heart which the silver coin in his pocket did not altogether explain.

## II. IN THE STUDY

It will be abundantly obvious from what has already been said that little room was left in Collier's crowded days for the life of the study. There is evidence that during the first four years of his ministry he worked at his books carefully and systematically ; [1] but from 1885 onwards, everything had to give way to the claims of the Manchester Mission. Nor was there, so far as I have been able to discover, either then or at any other time, any hesitation about the path he should

[1] For example, he writes (Aug. 12, 1917) to his son who was preparing for the ministry : ' It is well to keep ample records, analyses, references etc. I have lost an immense amount of useful material for lack of this systematic effort. The first four years I tried, and reap to-day the result ; that little has often saved me much labour. But when I go to Manchester I was compelled to give time, energy, thought to one great purpose—the founding of the Mission.'

follow. Of any struggle between rival and com-
peting interests, his friends saw no sign; there
were no lingering looks behind, no idle regrets for
what once might have been, and now could never
be. Rather, he gave one the impression that he
coveted no man's lot, that if he had had his years
to live over again, he would have made the same
choice; to this end was he born, to this end came
he into the world, that he might do the work
of the Manchester Mission. Nevertheless, Collier
knew as well as any man the place that books
and serious study ought to have in a minister's
life. He was never guilty of that unspeakably
foolish depreciation of learning into which the
evangelist has sometimes suffered himself to be be-
trayed. ' Surrender of the intellect ' indeed ! As
if—as Sir George Adam Smith says—religion did
not need all the brains we poor mortals can put
into it ! In a letter to his wife, full of a wise and
tender solicitude for the welfare of their four sons,
but too private to be given here, Collier writes of
the one who was destined for the Christian ministry :
' In giving him to the service of God, I would
like to give him at his best, a well-educated, refined, spiritually-minded and earnest, evangelistic
minister.' And the letter goes on to discuss the
necessary readjustments of the family budget in
order to secure for him a university course. ' I am
not over-anxious,' he says, ' nor am I worrying, but I
am desirous to do right at this juncture. We will
do all we can to give each of our lads a good chance

for this life and the next, for their own success, and for God's service.'

It ought to be said, too, that Collier managed to get a good deal more reading done than many of his brethren gave him credit for. For one thing he had, in a very unusual degree, the gift of picking other men's brains ; and as the work of the Mission, and particularly the Tuesday mid-day service, brought him into frequent contact with many of the foremost religious teachers and preachers of the land, he had unusual opportunities for exercising it. ' I have little time to forage for myself,' he used to say to his friends, ' tell me what there is good coming out.' He had learned, too, the meaning of the apostolic word about ' making the very most of the time '—ἐξαγοραζόμενοι τὸν καιρόν.[1] Most of his reading was done in bed and on holidays ; and as, fortunately, he was a fairly quick reader, he was able to get through what was, under the circumstances, a surprisingly large number of books. Once in a meeting of Free Church ministers, held at Union Chapel, Manchester, he told how it was done ; and I cannot do better than quote his own simple words : ' My days,' he said, ' are spent largely in the office and in committee, and it must be evident to my brethren that I could not have carried on the spiritual work of the Mission if there had not been another side to my life. God seems to have taken this matter into His own hands, knowing how fully every hour of my time is occupied.

[1] Eph. v. 16.

The desire and the need for long sleep seem to have been taken away from me. I cannot sleep early in the evening, but from twelve to two I generally sleep fairly well, then invariably I wake and there is no more sleep until six o'clock. At first I used all sorts of means to try to induce sleep, but by degrees I accepted the inevitable. I provided myself with a special light and a little table on which I kept a few favourite books, and in that way I get as much quiet reading as many of my brethren. The books I have on my table are those that are likely to help me in the deepening of my spiritual life. At six o'clock I sleep for an hour, and then get up ready for the day's work.'

As the words just quoted might suggest, Collier gave a large place in his reading and thinking to such subjects as Prayer and the Holy Spirit. When he prepared the hymn sheets for use in the Sunday services of the Mission, it was his custom always to include one hymn addressed to the Spirit.[1] He was always buying new books on Prayer; when Dr. Fosdick's well-known little book on that subject appeared, he presented a copy of it to each of the Sisters of the Mission. Of modern religious writers he owed most, perhaps, to Dr. M'Laren. Another favourite was Dr. W. M. Clow, of Glasgow. He was much impressed by Professor J. A. Robertson's *Spiritual Pilgrimage of Jesus*, and by Sir W. Robertson Nicoll's *Reunion in Eternity*, his copy of which showed signs of very careful reading. Among the

[1] See the incident related on p. 118,

older novelists he liked best Scott, Dickens, Thac-
keray, and George Eliot. Recent writers who
specially appealed to him were Ian Hay, A. A. Milne,
John Buchan, and W. J. Locke. Naturally he was
much interested in social problems, and he read
widely, though sometimes with more weariness than
profit, in Blue-books and the reports of conferences
and commissions.

But probably the subject which lay nearest his
heart, where books were concerned, was Hymnology.
He approached the subject, of course, mainly from
the practical point of view; that is to say, he
sought for hymns—and tunes—that would lend
effectiveness and power to popular worship. He
had on his shelves a large collection of hymns and
sacred songs, and he spent many hours ransacking
them for treasure with which to enrich his Sunday
services. He knew something of music—enough,
at least, to enable him to test the tunes for
himself. Not only so, but he knew what he
wanted, and what he believed the people wanted.
He thought, as Dr. Dale thought, and as many
others think, that the whole spirit of public worship
is often chilled and depressed by the use of hymns
which congregations find no delight in singing,
either because their language is stiff and cold, or
because they are set to tunes in which life and fire
have been sacrificed to correctness.[1] And so he

[1] In an old number of *The Congregationalist*—March 1875—there is a
very striking article written by Dr. Dale on the occasion of the first
visit of Moody and Sankey to Birmingham. I venture to disinter a few
sentences, partly for their own sake, but still more because I believe

waded through book after book, fitting tunes to hymns and hymns to tunes, in order that in the great congregation men and women might sing unto the Lord and make a joyful noise to the God of their salvation. Collier's interest in this subject led to his being invited to edit *The Free Church Council Hymnal*—' a Hymnal for use in Special Missions.' One hymn in the collection—number 28 —though his name is modestly omitted, is from his own pen.

they exactly represent Collier's own feeling about hymns and music in the worship of the Church :

' Sankey's " songs " have been sharply criticised. It is very easy to criticise them ; it might be more profitable to consider why it is that both the music and the words are so popular and effective. . . . The tunes which were sung by Nonconformist congregations thirty years ago were often vulgar, but they were real tunes, easily learnt, easily remembered ; and they haunted people during the week. Most of them were destitute of artistic merit, but the people liked them, and they were the natural expression of their emotion. Many of the new tunes are not " tunes " at all. They are not vulgar, but they are uninteresting. They differ from their predecessors very much as the dulness of a " respectable " dinner party differs from the merriment of a picnic, at which the people are just a little unrefined, but at which they have resolved to enjoy themselves. I do not like either, but on the whole I prefer the picnic. The men who have composed or adapted the new tunes are for the most part organists, who know very much more about how to get solemn effects out of their instrument than how to give the people something to sing. Mr. Sankey's melodies—whatever their demerits—are caught by thousands of people of all kinds, cultivated and uncultivated, men, women and children, and are sung " with a will."

' I agree with those who say that we ought, if possible, to get really good music for God's service, but it must be on one condition : that we do not sacrifice "God's service" to the "good music." Our first business is to enable Christian congregations to give free and happy expression to their joy and trust in God's love, and their reverence for God's majesty : the promotion of their musical taste is a matter of only secondary importance. . . . The same principles are applicable to Sankey's hymns. Critics have said that they are "childish," that they have no "literary merit," that there is something ridiculous in hearing a

### III. IN THE HOME

Among the many letters which Mrs. Collier received after the death of her husband was one from a distinguished minister of the Baptist Church, who said : ' My stays in your home are some of the sunshiny memories of my life. I don't know of a wife who had a husband who was more of a lover, or boys who had a father who was more of a companion.' These words truly and fitly sum up the little that needs to be said concerning Collier's life in the home.

He was married on April 23, 1889, to Miss Ettie

congregation of grown people singing with enthusiasm "I am so glad that Jesus loves me." Well, the fact that hymns that are simple even to childishness are sung by grown people with so much earnestness, that hymns with no "literary merit" kindle new fire in the hearts of men and women who know something of Shakespeare, Milton, and Wordsworth, is surely worth investigating. Is it the "childishness" which accounts for the power? Is it the absence of "literary merit"? I think not. Give the people a collection of hymns characterised by equal fervour, expressing with the same directness the elementary convictions and the deepest emotions of the Christian heart, and if they have also the literary merit which is absent from many, at least, of Mr. Sankey's songs, they will become equally popular, and their popularity will be more enduring. But our hymn books are too stiff and cold. People want to sing, not what they *think*, but what they *feel*; and if they are asked to sing hymns in which there is no glow of feeling, and in which the thought is perfectly commonplace, they will not sing at all. "I am so glad that Jesus loves me" is a childish way of expressing our joy in the love of Christ; but if hymn writers will not help us to express it in a more masculine way, we must express it as best we can. . . . Again, it is no use asking people to sing to God in a language remote from the language of their common life. . . . Mr. Binney's "Eternal Light" has the simplicity, fervour, and dignity which constitute a perfect hymn ; but I am not sure whether its dignity does not impose a kind of strain upon very many minds, which though very good for them occasionally, interferes with their delight in singing it.'

Collin, of Manchester. Mrs. Collier is still living (1923), and that alone would be sufficient to restrain, if restraint were needed, the writer's pen.

> ' Not easily forgiven
> Are those who, setting wide the doors that bar
> The secret bridal chambers of the heart,
> Let in the day.'

But by Mrs. Collier's kindness I have been permitted to read some of the letters addressed to her by her husband, and intended, of course, for no other eyes than hers ; and, though they are not for quotation here, there can be no harm, I think, in saying that they deepen the beauty of that lifelong honeymoon of which those who were privileged to know the Colliers' home must often have caught some glimpses. Among the very few complete manuscripts of any kind that Collier left behind him is one of the address delivered at the wedding of his eldest son. I give it here in full, because it sets forth the ideals that Collier had always before him during the two and thirty years of his own married life :—

> ' If our desires and hopes which find expression in our prayers are fulfilled, then your happiness and well-being are assured for all time. Our confidence is based on the fact that you both come to God's altar having consecrated your lives to Him. You have learned that all life is sacred, and will feel specially to-day and in the days to come the sanctity of married life. You will find there is in it great opportunity for mutual help. You have already had the privilege of a more intimate knowledge of each

other than ordinary friendship makes possible, and you will learn still more of each other's virtues and failings by the closer intercourse of married life. Though you may find limitations which you did not expect, or excellencies surpassing what you already know, I trust you will never be really disappointed in each other; and in learning to understand each other you may be mutually helpful. You will have a right to expect, and I am sure will show to each other, more sympathy, consideration and appreciation than you will get from any one else. In a common yearning after the true, the good, and the beautiful, in a unity of desire and ambition for the highest purposes of life, we pray you may succeed.

' I am sure you do not look upon happiness alone as the chief end of married life. There is no finer discipline in any walk of life than that of the home and family. There is ample opportunity for the development of character, and much depends on each for the perfecting of this discipline. It will be well for you to consider each other—not to be exacting, to be full of sympathy, and by patience and fidelity in love, to stand by each other. You will have new opportunities for service. Already in the Church and for the nation you have shown yourselves prepared to consecrate your gifts to God and man; together you will be more than ever equal to the calls of service. I would have you to note how often that word " together " occurs in the Marriage Service. It is together that you will face trial and difficulty; together you will share both joy and sorrow; together you will face life and build up your character and your home. The establishment of a Christian home will be one of the highest services

you will be able to render to the nation. Home
life is indeed the greatest national asset. A
unique opportunity lies before you, we pray
that your highest expectations may be fulfilled.'

Five children were born to Mr. and Mrs. Collier,
all of them sons, of whom one died in infancy, and
two were killed in the Great War. Only a few of
the father's letters to his boys have been preserved,
but sufficient to illustrate the genial companionship
in which he lived with them, and the affectionate
care with which he watched over and guided them.
The following was written to one of them whose
schooldays were drawing to a close, but whose
future was still undecided :—

'THE OLIVES, *Mar.* 13, 1909.

' MY DEAR HAROLD,—I have been thinking and
praying about you boys a good deal this week,
and feel I would like to write you a private note.
What about your future ? You will be leaving
at the end of next term. Then you will be
eighteen. This means you have had an extra
chance for preparation for the future, physically,
mentally, and spiritually. Do you still feel
called to the ministry ? Does your love for
Jesus Christ increase ? Do you still read and
think about your Bible ? Is prayer more *real*
to you day by day ? These questions will help
you to test yourself. What is your influence on
other boys ? Do they look up to you as a
Christian ? Do you influence them for good ?
Do you ever try to save them from wrong, and
try to win them for Christ ? I want you to
examine yourself prayerfully and carefully on

these points.  You are seventeen and a half years old and ought to stand for something now as a servant of Jesus Christ, especially if you are to be set apart for the ministry.  Of course, whatever you may be, you can serve Jesus in that sphere.  I am ambitious about your future, but my chief desire is that you should be a godly man.  I can honestly say I want you to be this above all things.  Think this letter over, and some time write me a private letter.  If you like you can address it to the Central Hall.  God bless you, Harold.  I have great desires for you. Hence this letter.  I trust you fully, and only want to help you by telling you what has been on my heart this week every day.—With earnest prayer for you always, I am, your loving

FATHER.'

To the same son, who eventually entered into business, he writes again at a later date :—

[Undated.]

' MY DEAR HAL,—I have been thinking a good deal about you in the early hours and I am now writing in bed.  I have prayed much daily for you lately.  You are passing through a time of testing, and I want to see you above all a man of faith and loyalty to Christ.  This is the most important of all.  Never get in the habit of blaming Providence.  It is as foolish and harmful as it is absurd.  And we all know it is so even when we do it.  God's character is above suspicion.  He has been specially good to us in our home and family comfort. . . . " Have faith in God."  I am sure all will come right for you, if you go straight, and act sensibly.

' Keep still on the look-out.  Don't go at it apologetically.  Make everybody feel you are keen, and determined to make the world bend before you. . . . Begin self-improvement as you think best. Every bit of *special* knowledge (shorthand, typing, languages, commercial economics, etc.), lifts a man out of the ruck of those who have nothing but a superficial and general knowledge ; it gives marketable value. Don't let pride hinder you from setting about things.

'A good time to you to-night at class. I am so glad you do that work. Stick to it, my boy, and all that is like it. I hope you can read this. It is written with my heart's best love.

FATHER.'

The following letters were addressed to a younger son, who is now in the ministry of his father's Church :—

'THE CENTRAL HALL,
*Nov.* 1, 1910.

'MY DEAR DONALD,—I 'm fearfully busy, but I feel I must send you a line to say how glad I was to receive your letter. Many, many thanks. It is a joy to me to feel that you can write so frankly. Yes, I know what your position is. I passed through a similar phase of school life. But responsibility is always good for us, and especially at your age. It quickens manhood, and it gives you an opportunity of standing for all that 's good. Even when the boys don't seem to like your stand, if you do all in the right spirit they will at heart honour you. I shall know now how better to pray for you. God be with you, my boy, and clear the way for you in coming days.—Much love,

FATHER.'

'THE CENTRAL HALL,
*Mar.* 18, 1911.

'MY DEAR DON,—I am glad you are taking a good position in the school, and with Mr. Beattie.[1] Your position is not an easy one. I know all about the difficulties, for I had exactly the same position at Bickerton House. You have a duty both to the boys and to Mr. Beattie. You can be a great blessing to the school. Stand for truth, purity, and all that is Christlike; do it in all humility, or, as you would say, "without side." You may at times feel as if you are likely to be misjudged, but keep straight and all will be well. God help, guide, and strengthen you! I hope soon to see you. Much love,

FATHER.'

'HARROGATE, *May* 29, 1911.

'MY DEAR DON,—I'm sorry to hear of this possible disappointment after you have worked so hard. But don't get "down"; all will be well. God has charge of your life. You have tried hard to do your duty, and I'm really proud of you. Many thanks for your letter of this morning. It did me good—a lot of good. Keep your faith strong in prayer. It's not weak but strong to lean hard on God. In haste. —Your affectionate                FATHER.'

'THE CENTRAL HALL,
*July* 8, 1911.

'MY DEAR DONALD,—This week I've been two days at Didsbury in the July Examination Committee for candidates for our ministry. It is a very interesting Committee. There were about sixty young men, and we passed thirty-eight of them. I could not help thinking of you

[1] The Headmaster.

all the time, and wondering how soon you would be in that position. There were three or four ministers' sons, and two of the best candidates were among these. I offered many a prayer for the fellows, and your name came into my prayers that God would fit you every day for your great future as His minister. Keep that before you—*His* minister. In every way try to fit yourself as well as ask Him to fit you. Fit yourself physically, mentally, spiritually; set before yourself a life of very high principle, a great ideal, and live it daily by God's help. I cannot tell you how ambitious I am for you, and how I place my highest hopes in you. . . .— Love from all, FATHER.'

'COLLINWOOD, DEGANWY,
*Aug.* 12, 1917.

'MY DEAR DONALD,—With a heart full of love for you I wish you very many happy returns of the day. May God spare you for a happy and successful ministry! It has been a great satisfaction and joy to me that He has called you into His ministry, and that you responded to the call. So far you have had a fuller ex-perience than mine or many others. You had ample opportunity in preparation of body and mind at school and university; a year at Didsbury; then out into the war-time experi-ence of chaplain. Who could have foreseen all this? And how wonderfully God has pre-served your life! I believe in time He will give you back your health; that is my daily prayer, and for this great purpose—that you may fulfil to the full your great calling. The present years are very precious ones in prepara-tion by reading, experience, and communion with the Divine. You will never have the same chance again, for the years all seem to bring an increase of *detailed* work that robs one of the same opportunities. . . . Well, I believe you will be guided aright. If our daily prayers are answered for you, you will be rich indeed. Above all I earnestly pray that the holy life without which no man can have the influence he ought to have may be yours.

'We are eagerly awaiting your coming. Mother and I have tried to think of a birthday present, and failed to come to a satisfactory decision. The money is here and you must decide when you arrive.

'I preached this morning at Bethel on Psalm lxii. 8.

'We are proud of you and our hearts are full as we talk of you to-day.

'Fondest love from mother and self,

FATHER.'

Collier's was always a happy nature—'no lark more blithe than he '—and it was in his home, with his wife and boys, that his happiness was at its height. Except, too, for the death of his infant son in 1897,[1] the years had dealt kindly with him and his. Then came the vast shadow of the Great War which darkened all the land, and turned his day into night. Twice in one week the desolating stroke fell which carried off both his eldest and his youngest sons. It was a cruel, staggering blow ; nevertheless, he went bravely on. Hearts were breaking all around him, and for their sakes he

[1] It is worth noting that on the Sunday when his babe lay dead in the house he preached twice as usual. His wife asked him if he thought he could manage it. 'Ettie,' he said, 'if I were a working-man I'd have to go to work just the same. I mustn't shirk my duty.'

dare not let sorrow work its wild will upon him. Yet he was never quite the same man again. ' This is our passion week,' he wrote to an old friend one year when the anniversary of his boys' death fell in Holy Week. Again and again, when he was in Australia, he would say, ' Wouldn't Sidney '— Sidney was his Benjamin—' have loved to be here now ? ' or, ' Sidney would have had something to say about this.' Only a fortnight before his own death he said to another of his sons, ' I never have them out of my mind for long. But there is always one day each week when they are constantly in my thoughts, and I can't help feeling the pity of it all.' He made no parade of pain ; but he went about like a man deeply wounded, whose wound bled inwardly.

### IV. IN THE SECRET PLACE

' Your father,' Collier once wrote to the Rev. W. Bardsley Brash, ' had the two characteristics I covet most for myself, sanity and spirituality.' [1] No one ever questioned Collier's sanity ; it impressed the most casual observer. He had indeed an almost uncanny shrewdness in fitting means to ends in every form of Christian service. But the other coveted quality men were not so quick to recognise in him. Nevertheless, it was there, and it was there in fuller measure than those who only saw him at a distance perhaps ever guessed. There

---

[1] The story of the father, the Rev. J. Denholm Brash, is told in his son's delightful biography of him entitled *Love and Life.*

could not but be peril in a life so crowded as his;
fortunately, he knew it, and therein lay his safe-
guard. He was walking home one day with a
younger preacher, whose popular gifts were just
beginning to attract large crowds : ' I say, ——,'
he said, ' have you ever thought of that text, *Great
multitudes came together to hear. But He withdrew
Himself in the deserts, and prayed* ' ? It was a word
of counsel to his companion ; but it was still more
a word about himself, and his own conscious daily
need. The truth is, Collier was something of a
mystic ; a ' practical mystic ' indeed, to borrow
Lord Rosebery's happy phrase about Oliver Crom-
well, but still a mystic. What Lord Morley says
of Gladstone, that he ' lived from a great depth of
being,' was true also in its way of Collier. All his
springs were in God. A favourite text, which
hung for years in his office in the Central Hall, was
this : *God is able to make all grace abound unto you ;
that ye, having always all sufficiency in all things, may
abound unto every good work.* The full, rushing
stream of his daily activities was fed from the
eternal hills.

> ' Firm faith, and evermore
> Prayer from a living source within the will,
> And beating up through all the bitter world,
> Like fountains of sweet water in the sea,
> Kept him a living soul.'

What has been said earlier in this chapter about
Collier's reading shows his interest in the mystical,
experimental side of religion ; but beyond this he
had schooled himself to be ' alone with the Alone,'

to push back the throng and press of things, and to make a space about himself where he might have room for quiet and thought and prayer. The casual acquaintance rarely saw this side of the man; perhaps he hardly suspected it. He knew his tremendous powers of work, he laughed at his merry stories, and went away saying what a terrific worker he was, and what a jolly good fellow, but knowing the secret neither of his labour nor his laughter. But those who were privileged to be near him knew. 'He was always ready,' one of his oldest friends in the work of the Mission once said to me, 'for deep soul-talk.' 'When we went away together, as we often did,' says Dr. J. A. Hutton, 'our talk was rarely of the merely external side of his work, but of the inner side—of the moods favourable or sinister in the public mind towards the faith.' 'There was no man,' Dr. Campbell Morgan writes, 'to whom I went, in hours of personal perplexity on all sorts of subjects, with more assurance that a long, quiet talk with him would enable me to see a situation completely and clearly, than S. F. Collier. I always felt that in converse with him I had been brought very near to the mind of Christ.' The greatest hour in the day for some of his fellow-workers was when he met them for prayer, morning by morning, at the Central Hall. A few lines from a letter to his wife —June 20, 1910—may help us to understand why : 'I 've a lot to think about just now and feel the responsibility more than I sometimes care to say.

If I could not say, " I believe in God, *the Father* Almighty," and realise the truth of His guidance, care, and over-ruling Providence, I should not dare to go on with my work.   Christian work is not easier, conditions of the people are perplexing, one's own life grows in bigness and responsibility, and one feels more what it means to live as one gets older. I remember always the Master's answer to His perplexed disciples, *Have faith in God.*   Now I must stop this or you 'll think I am sermonising.   But I am not ;  I 'm just emptying my mind in yours by way of relief.   There are things that can't be said to everybody.   The life in Christ is the only one worth living, and it is worth everything else.'

And when the worst storm of his life struck him, his faith still held.   One or two tiny memories of that sad time will show what I mean.   ' The morning after Sidney was killed,' [1] writes one of the Sisters of the Mission, ' Mr. Collier came down [to the Hall] to take prayers as usual.   He commenced to read the Psalm, but broke down and had to leave the room.   Mr. Crook, the late treasurer of the Mission, continued to read, but before he finished, Mr. Collier returned and led in prayer without a break in his voice.'   ' I heard him preach,' writes another correspondent, ' the Sunday in March 1918, two days before he got the telegram telling him of his son Sidney's death.   His subject

---

[1] It should be explained that Collier's youngest son, Sidney, was reported ' killed ' at once ; his eldest son, Frank, was at first, and for long, only reported ' missing.'

was " The Anchor that holds." The Sunday following I heard him again. I shall never forget how
he tried to be as cheerful and encouraging as usual,
telling us if his son could speak he would say,
" Carry on." He alluded to his sermon of the
previous Sunday and said, " I little thought how
soon I would be called upon to trust to that
Anchor. I am here to-night to tell you, it *does*
hold." ' It was a frequent way of Collier's to end
letters to his friends with the words ' *Laus Deo* '—
' Praise to God.' When his sons' funeral cards had
to be prepared it did not seem either suitable or
sufficient to write the usual ' In Memoriam ';
instead he wrote, even there, the old, happy ' *Laus
Deo*.' And when his own turn came those who
loved him wrote again, ' In praise to God.'

# CHAPTER X

## PRESIDENT OF THE CONFERENCE

### 1913–1914

THE first ' Yearly Conference of the People called Methodists '—to use the familiar and time-honoured phraseology—was held in 1744. As long as John Wesley was alive there was, of course, only one possible President. Since his death in 1791 his chair has been filled by a succession of Methodist preachers annually elected by the vote of their ministerial brethren.[1] Men of very varying types have been chosen for the high honour : preachers like Morley Punshon, scholars like William F. Moulton, evangelists like Charles Garrett, administrators like James H. Rigg, and a few of manifold gifts like Hugh Price Hughes. Often, far too often indeed, the honour has been deferred until the recipient was well on in his sixties, and his physical strength unequal to the tremendous strain which, under present-day conditions, the presidential office inevitably imposes. Fortunately for himself, and for his Church, Collier was only fifty-seven when, at Liverpool in 1912, he was designated to

[1] Oddly enough, in these democratic days, this restriction to the ministerial members of the Conference of the right to elect the President is still maintained in English Wesleyan Methodism. Use and wont is all that can now be pleaded in defence of a practice which has long been abolished in all the other Methodist Churches throughout the world.

succeed his old college friend, F. Luke Wiseman, in the chair of the Wesleyan Methodist Conference. A brief note, written to his wife immediately after the vote had been declared, reveals his own feeling about the honour and responsibility which had come to him : ' You know,' he said, ' I have not sought the honour at all, and indeed have shrunk from it. I'm glad for your sake, and for the sake of the boys, and of special friends who desire to see me President. Now I rely on God's help. I have prayed that He would only permit this election if He meant to go with me all the way.'

The Conference of 1913 met at Plymouth. One of the first and most important duties of the newly-elected President is the delivery of his two inaugural addresses—the first to the Representative Session, the second, a week later, to the Pastoral Session. There were the usual little pleasantries as the retiring President handed over to his successor the simple insignia of his office. Of course, Collier must have his bit of fun : ' No one expected me to occupy the chair,' he said, glancing back to their Didsbury days together; ' everybody knew you would.' ' I do not profess to be a Wiseman,' he went on ; ' I am only a Collier ; but I've never been a Collier on strike or out of employment.' Then he turned to the serious business of his address —' Wesleyan Methodism and its Message for To-day.' It was, like that to his fellow-ministers the following week, both in matter and in manner, wholly characteristic of the man. On the literary side it answered to Mr. Augustine Birrell's description of the kind of speeches the House of Commons likes to listen to to-day : ' Plain, lucid statements, gathering up all the arguments, the right word, the clean phrase, and no frills.' Probably not a few of the members of the Conference were surprised at the character and frequency of the literary allusions. This busy man of affairs was evidently not such a stranger in the world of books as some of them had imagined. It was not merely that he quoted Methodist writers, and famous divines like Chalmers, Martineau, Dale, Liddon, and M'Laren ; Wordsworth, Mark Pattison, R. L. Stevenson, Sir James Paget, Sir J. R. Seeley, and Grant Robertson were all pressed into his service. In their subject-matter, Collier's two presidential addresses were simply the philosophy of his own life and work, the reduction to theory of his twenty-eight years' practice in the Manchester Mission. As this has been abundantly illustrated in the foregoing pages, nothing further need be said about it here. But a brief quotation dealing with two other points will, I think, be of interest.

When the Conference met in Plymouth the peace of the Wesleyan Methodist Church was seriously threatened by a sharp theological controversy which had broken out during the preceding year. Pamphleteers and newspaper correspondents had been waging a fierce warfare, and nobody quite knew how the matter might end. The President, of course, could side with neither party, but his wise words from the chair did much to bring about the all but unanimous decision which was eventually reached. First he pleaded for the note of certainty in the Methodist pulpit :—

> ' Too many are busy dissecting, others defending, the Gospel, when they ought to be heralding it with triumphant certainty. Men are tired of negative criticism—of teaching that neither strengthens faith, confirms hope, creates enthusiasm, nor comforts the soul. They are often amused at the satisfaction with which we quote any scientist or psychologist who deigns to patronise Jesus Christ, or has written a testimony to the probable efficacy of prayer, as if we were not certain of our own convictions. If our experience has not produced conviction for ourselves and the note of certainty in our witness, no amount of outside testimony of this sort will give power to our message. We are witnesses of these things. Our appeal will be effective in the measure that we are evidently sure of what we preach and what we testify.'

But, he went on :—

> ' This does not mean that the spirit of Methodism is intolerant of criticism and research. As long as we are loyal to the Evangel, " never too broad for the Cross's narrow way," Methodism, like her founder, cramps no man's mental outlook. There is far more liberty of thought in our Church than is generally supposed. Joseph Benson's letter to a critic expresses the mind of Wesley, who is said to have inspired the letter : " I never undertook to defend every sentence of Mr. Wesley's. He does not expect it or desire it. He wishes me, and every man, to think for himself." '

The other feature of Collier's opening address was its frank, outspoken counsel to the laity; he was equally outspoken, be it remembered, in his address to the ministers a week later :—

> ' When the laity fail to fulfil their responsibility they are creating ecclesiasticism—the minister is compelled to undertake the duties that ought to be in the hands of the laity, and develops into the ecclesiastic against his will. It is said that in many circuits ministers find it difficult to persuade men to take office ; they go, cap in hand, to beg men to fill the official positions in God's house.  Surely there is something wrong when a high privilege like this of serving God and His Church is shunned or treated as a burden ! . . . You may retire from your golf, your mill, your work, your club, but you must not retire from the business of Christ till He comes.  It is mockery to sing—
>
> > " Happy if with my latest breath
> > I may but gasp His name,"
>
> and talk of retiring at fifty.  Your young people will not believe in such a religion.  They are not going to accept seriously a religion at eighteen or twenty-one that you find less use for, and less interest in, as you get older.'

One testimony to the power of the address written while the first impression was still fresh is worth reproducing :—[1]

> ' It was a business-like performance ; it had the air of one who was not flustered, and was after something he much wanted ; of one who

From one of the Rev. Arthur Hoyle's brilliant Conference sketches in the *Methodist Recorder*.

knew that the thing he was after was to be got, if he could hit upon the way. But it was more than that. It had nothing of the tactician, of the committee man, of the administrator, nor much of the theologian; but it had plenty of salt, a most sound savour, a noble sanity and clarity, as tolerant as light. It was massive and yet beautiful; it was immensely practical, and yet imagination played and toyed with touches of literature—even with Matthew Arnold.[1] I don't quite know how to get at the heart of the message, save to say it was Methodism, neither old-fashioned nor new-fashioned, but just Methodism, and a brave, manly man speaking from his heart. . . . There was a quality I have not reached yet. Few men have said plainer things, things more significant of distressful habits and lamentable failures. He got home to " the depth of inbred sin," " the pride that lurks within." It was with a most monstrous directness he spake the truth. I can recall men who, if they had said those things, might have seen the Conference taking its hat and going home, turning away in anger, too proud to make reply. But these things were so said that they fell with a kind of healing balm. I know not how it was managed, but it *was* managed, that the truth was told bluntly, and yet it came home as your own children come home in innocence, and bring messages from one you love. I don't think it was a manner; it was a man. It was not attempted; it was never thought of. Out came the wholesome truth, and you saw the square figure in the unaccustomed place and understood why you had to hear these things,

[1] I fancy there must be a slip here; at least I can find no reference to Arnold in the address as it was afterwards printed.

and why you would have it all just so, and not otherwise.'

The extracts which have already been given [1] from Collier's second address from the Chair—that to the Pastoral Session—make any further quotation from it unnecessary ; but I am glad to be able to give an old colleague's testimony to the painstaking care with which the two addresses were prepared : ' A few weeks before Conference,' he writes, ' he sent me a post card asking me to call at the office, and when I got there I found that he wanted to read to me his two presidential addresses, which he did in full.  He said he would be most grateful if I would give him my frank opinion, as this kind of thing was a little out of his ordinary beat.  He felt he had a message to give, but he was most anxious it should be given in the right spirit and temper.  The address to his brethren in the Pastoral Session gave him much concern.  He felt it laid upon him to speak strongly on Ministerial Leadership, but was most anxious to do it in a brotherly spirit, and he asked me to pull him up if I thought that any phrase might be misunderstood or interpreted in a different spirit from the one in which he intended it to be taken.'

In addition to these two addresses, it falls to the lot of every President of the Conference to deliver, a year later, as ex-President, the Charge to the newly-ordained ministers.  Collier fulfilled this final

---

[1] See pp. 70 and 97.

official duty at Leeds, in July 1914. A printed copy of
the Charge lies before me as I write. It is as simple,
as direct, as unpretentious, as Collier always knew
how to be. From beginning to end there is nothing
in it that is either novel or brilliant, either in the
thing said or in the way of saying it. But there is
something that is better than both—the gathered
wealth of the years coined into pithy and homely
speech. I quote a few of its ' rugged maxims,' all
of them learned and tested in the hard school of
life :—

> ' All vocations have their peculiar perils. No
> vocation is beset with more subtle temptations
> than the ministry—temptations of the study,
> pulpit, home, social life. We need to be on our
> guard lest we become *godless in the service of
> God.*'
> ' Familiarity with sacred things may prove
> our undoing. We may talk theoretically about
> religious experiences when we have ceased to
> enjoy them ourselves. We may deceive our-
> selves into thinking we possess what we so often
> talk about ; exhort to pray, and pray little
> ourselves ; plead for the study of God's Word,
> and make little use of it devotionally ; persuade
> to service and to witness, while we are lazy and
> indifferent in our own life. Beware of losing
> the sense of reality in your ministry.'
> ' Beware of the peculiar temptations of social
> life. The open door into the homes of our
> members, the friendly terms on which we may
> be, the enjoyment of recreation with them, the
> generous kindness of the laity, all mean peril
> to us if we are not careful to remember that
> we are first the minister, then the friend. We

may be both, but we must, for our work's sake, make up our mind that nothing in the relationship shall hinder our life's purpose "by all means to save some." You may put yourself under such obligation that your independence is gone, and your mouth is muzzled.'

' We need to discipline ourselves in method, in habits of punctuality, accuracy, regularity, and the like, lest we waste our time and other people's. Let no business man say that he has better business habits than you, that he is more correct than you. He may be cleverer in business than you, but he ought not to be a rebuke to you in good, correct, reliable, business habits. Count your hours a sacred trust.'

One of the young ministers to whom the Charge was addressed acknowledged the receipt of a printed copy of it in the following letter :—

' May I thank you most heartily for this gift of your great Charge in this permanent form ? I am glad, however, that its most permanent form will be found in our ministries, for which your words were an inspiration. I am happy to think that I had a little share in requesting you to print it. Once again I have been studying the Charge, and again the words which were so deeply spoken from the heart have found my heart and searched my work. It is just what we needed, and I shall always be grateful for the message.'

Collier's conduct of the business of Conference called forth general approval, and not a little surprise. Until his election to the Chair he had taken little part in its proceedings. Moreover, as we have already seen, the Plymouth Conference had difficulties of its own.  A dropping barometer and the low mutterings of controversial thunder all round the horizon were a sure prophecy of trouble, unless the man at the wheel kept his head.  But there was never any need for anxiety.  The President's good temper and tact guided the Conference through the broken water of a long debate to a decision against which only seven hands were held up.  A still more difficult situation faced him in June of the following year when, according to the usual custom, he went to preside in the Irish Conference at Belfast.  The Government's Home Rule Bill, it will be remembered, was just about to be placed on the statute book.  Excitement in the North of Ireland was at fever-point.  There had been a tumultuous scene, only two weeks before, in the General Assembly of the Presbyterian Church. In the Methodist Church opinion was sharply divided.  ' It is safe to say,' writes an Irish correspondent, ' that not two per cent. of the ministers of the Irish Conference wanted any change of government.  They had lived under British rule from birth, and felt as individuals no hardships nor hindrances.'  Not only so, most of the older ministers of the Church, together with an overwhelming majority of the laity, were vehemently opposed to the proposals which now seemed on the point of becoming law.  On the other hand, there was a growing feeling among the younger ministers that the demand of the South of Ireland for self-government could no longer be met with a policy

of blind and blank resistance. Such was the
position: 'One party felt it was a time for patience
and caution in new and uncertain conditions; the
other felt that hesitation or caution meant betrayal
of all that was precious. A word might lead to
lasting bitterness, and a spark might set our Church
ablaze with unholy fire. When the hour struck
at which Irish Methodism was to declare itself on
the Irish Question, the Conference Hall in Belfast
was packed to overflowing. It was known a
strongly-worded resolution had been prepared—too
strong for the younger men to support. Would it
force a split? The deputation to commend the
resolution was received and heard. Then Mr.
Collier rose to his feet, his eye gleaming, but his
self-control easy and perfect. He spoke a few
moderating sentences, when some one interrupted
from the gallery. In an instant he transfixed his
interrupter with the question, "Are you a member
of this Conference?" and added, "If a second
interruption occurs I shall clear the gallery of all
who are not Conference members." Nothing needed
to be added. Then in a calm, judicial manner he
reviewed the situation as it appeared to him. What
would a strongly-worded resolution do? He wanted
light, and if any helpful word could be spoken, this
was the hour. They were above all things servant
of Christ. Could they not rise to a common level
in Christ, where all could unite? The brotherhood
of Methodism was very real; it had stood many a
strain, it would stand this also. As he spoke th

atmosphere changed perceptibly. Here was a man of God and a master of assemblies. We felt sobered, calmed, subdued, reasonable.' In the changed atmosphere another and more moderately worded resolution was brought forward, and in the end carried almost unanimously ; Gipsy Smith led the Conference in prayer and the session ended. ' Things have moved far and rapidly in Ireland since then,' continues the same correspondent, ' but two things stand out as one looks back over nine years as matters for thanksgiving. First, the Irish Methodist brotherhood stood the strain of divided opinions. No bitter feelings remained. Never were the members of its ministry more united, loyal, and affectionate. It might easily have been otherwise. Secondly, under God, Samuel F. Collier was the agent sent to guide the Conference into paths of peace and righteousness. He has gone to God, but his patience, wisdom, and moderating influence abide in Irish Methodism to this day, and in no part of the United Kingdom are his noble services more gratefully remembered than among the Irish people called Methodists.'

A letter to his wife indicates the relief which Collier felt when the fateful day was safely passed :—

> ' I tried to write you a letter in time for yesterday's afternoon post, but failed. I was kept very busily engaged every minute, and on the strain. We received a big deputation of laymen from all parts of Ireland in the morning, and then proceeded with a resolution on Home Rule. This continued until lunch time. We

closed with the vote before the end of the
morning sitting.　There was a full Conference,
and every moment the possibility of an explosion.
It reminded me of the morning at Plymouth
on the —— controversy.　You will, I know,
be glad to hear that yesterday's discussion
passed off as successfully as the Plymouth one.
I was thanked on all hands, and by both parties,
for the way I had managed the business.　I am
grateful to God for His help.　It seems strange
that I should have had two experiences of this
kind.　Yesterday there was not a sentence that
needs to be regretted.　That is saying a good deal,
for there wasn't a moment when heat could not
have been generated.　These Irishmen are feeling very deeply on this Home Rule question.'

There is a long and heavy list of public engagements which every President is expected to get
through during his year of office.　If, in addition to
these, he feels some special form of service laid upon
him, he can always count upon the loyal co-operation of the Methodist people.　Collier decided to
mark his term of office by a ' Campaign of Aggressive Evangelism.'　By this he did not mean a series
of evangelistic services—that he thought might
come later ;　his aim was rather the re-kindling of
the evangelistic spirit in the Churches themselves.
No man had toiled harder than he at the problems
of social reform, but he believed that behind and
beneath every other problem lies always the problem of the individual, and in this campaign he set
himself to lay afresh upon the mind and heart of
his Church the burden of souls.　' The supreme

duty of the Church of Christ,' he said, ' is the duty of preaching the Gospel.  Nothing else can take its place.  If it fails here, its own life declines and its influence on the world declines.  And if the Church is to preach the Gospel with effect, its own faith and vigour must be maintained at full strength. That is why I call this a campaign of evangelism. It is meant to put new life into the Churches themselves, to bring back their faith in their own mission. Unless they believe in themselves and feel that their message is of vital importance, how can they make any great impression on the world ? '

Gipsy Smith, Collier's old friend and fellow-campaigner, joined him, and together the two men visited every part of the country.  Great crowds welcomed them everywhere.  In Cornwall, for example, Collier calculated that within a few days they had addressed not less than 20,000 people. It is easy to ask, of course, like the little child in Southey's poem, ' But what good came of it at last ? '—and very difficult to answer.  When Collier's campaign began, the tide was out in all the Churches.  Almost before it was over the nation had plunged into the vortex of the Great War.  If to-day the tide is turning—and there are many signs that it is—something may be set down, at least in Methodism, to the patient persistence with which, not only during his Presidential year, but throughout his whole ministry, Collier proclaimed, by word and by deed, the primacy of the Church's obligation to evangelise.

Perhaps no incident of the campaign gave Collier greater personal satisfaction than his visit to his native town of Runcorn. Besides the usual public services, there were a presentation by old friends, a welcome by the local Free Church Council, and a civic luncheon given by the Chairman of the Urban District Council (Mr. R. H. Posnett). The health of the guest was proposed by his old school-fellow, Sir Frederick J. Norman, who spoke of him as the biggest man that Runcorn had ever bred.[1] Collier was never a man to set too great store by the generous things said of him by others, but this was an occasion of which he did right to be proud, and he went through the day, as some one observed at the time, in a singularly exalted mood.

Meanwhile, he was still carrying the burden of the Mission. The ceaseless round of public meetings, trying as it would have been to most men, was probably not more exacting to him than the strenuous activities which had been his normal life for so many years. He was, of course, often hard pressed. For the first time in his life he was driven to the dictation of letters on Sunday. Nevertheless, he managed, somehow or other, to keep in touch with things in Manchester. He made a point, whenever possible, of being at home on Monday in order that he might meet his workers in the usual staff meeting on Tuesday. And always he

[1] A bigger compliment than the uninstructed might perhaps suppose if, as the speaker claimed, Runcorn has had the bringing up, among others, of Southerne, the dramatist, Sir J. Rigby, the lawyer, Hall Caine, the novelist, and Arthur Nowell, the artist.

was his old, merry, resourceful self. When his year of office was over, there seemed no reason why he might not anticipate at least another dozen years of happy, fruitful service in Manchester. But, alas! the very month in which he became ex-President saw the piling up of the black thunder cloud of war; while it hung there, for him as for others, all life was changed; when it had lifted, his house was left unto him desolate.

# CHAPTER XI

## VISIT TO AUSTRALIA

### 1920–1921

ONLY once during the whole of the thirty-six years of Collier's superintendency of the Manchester Mission was he absent from it for more than a few weeks together. It happened, however, that the close of his Presidential year coincided with the celebration of the centenary of Methodism in Australia. It was natural, therefore, that he should be invited to be the bearer of the mother church's congratulations and goodwill to her many children under the Southern Cross. War intervened, and for the moment nothing came of the proposal. But at the Conference of 1919, at the urgent request of the Church in Australia, the invitation was renewed, and Collier agreed to go. He did so, however, with a good deal of reluctance and misgiving. For one thing, he had not, and he knew he had not, the kind of gifts that enable a man to shine as an ' occasional ' speaker. And then there was the Mission which lay on his heart by day and by night —could he afford to be away from it so long ? Some words from a letter to his friend Dr. Campbell Morgan (November 24, 1919) show how his mind was working : ' I am appointed as Methodist delegate (the first they have had) for Australia, and shall probably have to leave here about the middle of next July, and take Australia and Tasmania in the months of September, October, and November. The idea is to visit all the principal centres. I am not at all keen on going, but the Australian Conference asked for me, and our Conference would not listen to any protest on my part. My friends tell me it will add years to my life. Is there any special advantage in that ? We sing, " Earth 's but a sorry tent," and—

> " Ah me, ah me, that I
> In Kedar's tents here stay ! " '

What helped to reconcile him to his task was the hope that the long sea voyage might do something to restore the health of his wife, which had suffered seriously under the terrible strain of the years of war. With their son, the Rev. Donald Collier, they left Southampton for New York on June 16, 1920. Collier was greatly cheered by a kindly word of remembrance addressed to him from Downing Street by the Prime Minister. ' I have only just heard,' wrote Mr. Lloyd George, ' that you are shortly leaving this country, and I am taking the opportunity of writing to express the great admiration which I feel for the splendid work, both social and philanthropic, which you have carried on during the past thirty-five years. I am glad that you have undertaken to visit Australia and New Zealand, and feel sure, judging from the wide spiritual influence which you have exercised here, that these colonies cannot fail to benefit greatly by your mission.'

The travellers journeyed to the Pacific *via* the United States and Canada. Collier preached *en route* at Syracuse (New York), in the University Church there, at Winnipeg, where after the evening service he addressed an immense open-air meeting in Fort Rouge Park—' a great sight and a big opportunity '—and at Vancouver. A little incident at Syracuse gave him both some amusement and some satisfaction. He stopped some boys on the street to inquire for a house which he was seeking. It was pointed out to him. Then one of the boys said to him, ' Weren't you the preacher on Sunday ? My ! ' he went on, ' but you preached fine. I understood everything you said.' Perhaps the small boys of Syracuse do not usually presume to understand what is said from their University pulpit ! At Vancouver the Colliers embarked for Auckland, New Zealand. The long journey through the South Pacific was pleasantly varied by brief calls at Honolulu and the Fiji Islands. At Honolulu, where, through the kindness of an old college chum, the way had been prepared before him, Collier had his first glimpse of the gorgeous splendours of the Tropics :—

> ' every day
> The sunrise broken into scarlet shafts
> Among the palms and ferns and precipices ;
> The blaze upon the waters to the east ;
> The blaze upon the island overhead ;
> The blaze upon the waters to the west ;

Then the great stars that globed themselves in Heaven,
The hollower-bellowing ocean, and again
The scarlet shafts of sunrise.'

' At Fiji,' Collier wrote, ' we had a great welcome, the choir and members of the Jubilee Church coming to meet us. Unfortunately, the *Niagara* did not arrive till 11 P.M. The Fijians are not allowed in the streets after that hour without special permit, and they had to return home. They and we were disappointed. The minister, the head chief, and other Fijians who formed the Committee (for whom special permission had been obtained) remained to welcome us. We all went to the manse, and the ceremony, intended for the church, was held there. An address in Fijian was presented, the minister acting as interpreter for them, and for me in reply. They also presented me with a whale's tooth—a custom they have in recognition of any special guest they wish to honour. They gave the Prince of Wales two or three whale's teeth. It was all very kindly and very interesting. We left them soon after midnight.' They landed at Auckland on August 10.

From this day forward, until he left for home on December 10, Collier's life was one endless programme of public engagements, first in New Zealand, then in Australia and Tasmania. Wherever he went he experienced that abounding hospitality— to a modest man sometimes almost embarrassing in its generosity—which our kinsmen overseas so well know how to show to a visitor from the motherland.

But in Collier's case the welcome was not simply for the official delegate of British Methodism, but for the founder of a great work whose praise was in all the Churches of the English-speaking world. Everywhere the fame of his work had gone before him; everywhere civic receptions, luncheons, interviewers, audiences were waiting for him. Unfortunately, Collier kept no diary of his tour, he wrote but few letters, and all that remains for the hungry eyes of his biographer is a sheaf of newspaper cuttings out of which is now wholly gone whatever little virtue may once have been in them. After his return there were the inevitable interviews and speeches, and from these, as well as from his correspondence, some idea may be gained of the impression made upon him by all that he saw and heard. Himself an ardent admirer of Lloyd George, he noted with satisfaction the immense enthusiasm for that statesman in which all classes seemed to share. He was humbled by the wealth of personal kindness which Australians everywhere showered upon him; he felt the contagion of their cheerful optimism; he rejoiced in their passionate loyalty to the British throne, and in the vast potentialities of their young and vigorous realm. But there were other things that impressed him less favourably. He observed, he thought, a note of insularity, the result of Australia's remoteness from the rest of the world. The open-air life of the people at almost all seasons of the year, which their climate makes possible, seemed to him to be reacting prejudicially on the life of the home. On the subject of gambling, he declared, they had no conscience at all. ' I found,' he said, ' that when I spoke about drink at a meeting, the audience would listen with interest and approval ; but when I touched upon the evil of gambling there was an ominous silence.' The Methodism of Australia differs from that of the old land in various ways, both for better and for worse. Collier was much impressed by its energy, its influence on the life of the young Common-wealth, and the growing number of its laymen who were taking their part in public affairs. On the other hand, the loss of the class-meeting, he thought, had not only robbed it of its most char-acteristic institution, it had left a gap in its organ-isation which nothing could make good. Such were some of the opinions which Collier reported on his return to England. It seems right to give them a place in this brief chapter, but they need not be taken too seriously. One can hardly judge a continent on the strength of a four-months' tour, and it may well be that longer observation and fuller knowledge might have considerably modified some at least of these tentative conclusions.[1]

Throughout the whole of his journey nothing so cheered and warmed Collier's heart as the evidences

[1] Of course he kept his ears open for any addition to his stock of good stories. Here is one in the form in which it appears in one of his few Australian letters : A tourist party—grand mountain scenery—American in the party : ' Wal, this beats hell.' Englishman : ' How these Americans do travel !'

which it afforded of the far-reaching influence of
the Manchester Mission.   Again and again, wherever he went, he came across men and women
whose happiest, holiest memories were of the
Central Hall and of the new, redemptive power
which, through its services, had come into their
lives.   In several cases those who greeted him had
passed through the Homes and Shelters of the
Mission.   Others, who had served their apprentice-
ship under him as voluntary workers, were now
in the ranks of the Christian ministry.   One man
whom he met in Australia told him an odd story
of how, years before, he had gone one night drunk
to the Central Hall, how he had been shut up in
a room where there was a stuffed alligator—some
one's gift to a forthcoming ' Sale of Work '—and
how on rousing from his drunken stupor the sight
of the uncanny monster had almost frightened him
out of his wits !   In Sydney, two young married
women, who had seen his ' dear old face ' in the
morning paper, rushed down to the landing-stage
to be the first to greet him when he stepped on shore.
On his way home, he called for a few hours at
Colombo, Ceylon, where he was persuaded to conduct a brief service.   In the congregation, immediately behind Mrs. Collier, a woman sat, sobbing
for joy, completely overcome by her emotion at
seeing again her old pastor and friend.   And others,
who had no opportunity of seeing or hearing him,
wrote simple, heart-moving letters to bid him
welcome to Australia, and still more to tell him

how much through him God had done for them.
' You will find this a beautiful country, with any
amount of sunshine,' wrote one lonely woman,
who with her husband—since killed in the War—
had gone out to Australia eight years before; ' a
beautiful country, with any amount of sunshine.
I love the sunshine,' she went on, ' but I do not
forget dear, dirty old Manchester.'

And not old friends only did he find in Australia,
but troops of new ones.  At the outset, many who
heard him were disappointed :  his manner of
speaking seemed so casual, so unadorned and
matter-of-fact.  And, as this brief record must by
now have made abundantly clear, Collier had no
gifts of the showy, spectacular order.  But, as
one who himself experienced the initial disappointment goes on to say, presently those who listened
to him woke up to the discovery that he was ' throw-
ing down handfuls of nuggets before them.'  And
the longer they listened the deeper grew their
appreciation alike of the man and of his methods.
The Rev. Henry Howard, one of whose memories
of Collier's Australian visit has found a place on
an earlier page,[1] writes :—

> ' Collier had not the *ad captandum* gifts that
> tickle the crowd, and appeal to the sensation-
> monger.  But to those who could construe him
> through the work he had done, and listened to
> him with the memories of Manchester in their
> minds, he was all and more that they could

[1] See p. 92.

desire. The impression that he gave everywhere was that he was a great man for the job —calm, resolute, resourceful, with a wonderful sagacity, and a trustworthiness that won the most utter and immediate confidence. He greatly impressed every one with the absolute self-detachment with which he talked of his great work. Australians have always had their eye on the Manchester Mission. It has touched their imagination, and to have its missioner in the flesh, speaking to them in great, loving words, about the problems that are after all the same the whole world round—though intensified perhaps in England's great centres, as in no other place—was a joy too deep for words. Our hearts went out to him in a full tide of warm and welcoming love ; and to that love he responded, great human that he was, as few men could do, and gave us of his best. Even those who had not known him, or his work, could easily understand how such a great-heart won his way to the affection of the multitude, and made the Manchester Mission such a praise in the earth. Of course, he ought not to have had so much work thrust upon him, for he was a tired man. It was not as though he had got clear of the Mission while he was away. As I think I have said before, he never stood from under its weight, night or day; it was always in his thoughts. If you came upon him suddenly while he was brooding, the thought was always " Manchester." Like Goldsmith's " Traveller," he could say,

> " Where'er I roam, whatever realms to see,
> My heart untravell'd fondly turns to thee."

Sometimes I rallied him on it, but it was no use. Manchester was written on his heart, and held all the strongholds of his mind, so that even the gates of all Australia could not prevail against it. He greatly helped us all by his wise and brotherly counsel, and made us feel that we were on the winning side, who were fighting for the cause of righteousness and the coming of the Kingdom of God.'

The pity of it is, as Mr. Howard himself recognises, that Collier was led to undertake so heavy a programme. In saying this I am not blaming any one, least of all his generous Australian hosts. It was only natural that they should wish to make the most of his visit. Nevertheless, the fact remains that their eagerness to hear him, joined to his own readiness to serve them, led him sorely to overtax his strength. The journeys both in New Zealand and in Australia were longer than he had realised —for example, six or seven of his fourteen days in New Zealand were spent in travelling—and it is rather ominous to find him writing, only a fortnight after his landing in Auckland : ' I keep quite fit, though a little tired with constant travelling and daily meetings.' During his first week in Australia he spent one night and two days in the train, and preached or spoke seven times. By November 9, he calculated that he had already travelled 5500 miles, and spoken on over seventy occasions. Every letter home tells the same tale of long journeys, incessant speaking, and growing weariness : ' There is scarcely any opportunity for privacy in this constant rush,' he wrote ; ' I do not seem to have had a quiet hour since landing in Australia.'

There is no need to say more. Nature does not pay at the end of every week, but at last she pays ; and when, a few months later, Collier was attacked by disease, the reserves of strength which should have been there to meet it were all exhausted.

He reached England early in February 1921.

# CHAPTER XII

## CLOSING DAYS

### 1921

COLLIER's own people gave him a royal reception on his return to Manchester. His absence, said one of the speakers at his welcome meeting, had seemed like the disappearance of a familiar landmark from the city. But more striking than anything said from the platform was the sight of the great crowd of members and friends of the Mission which thronged the Albert Hall. A lady writing to Mrs. Collier a few months later, on the day after her husband's death, said : ' Our thoughts have been with you—and him—all to-day since we saw the paper this morning. And as I thought, the picture in my mind was always the same—the long queue of people waiting to get into the Albert Hall to the evening meeting to welcome you both back from Australia. Women in shawls and clogs, men on crutches, old and young of every sort, and all there because Mr. Collier was their friend.'

Then he plunged into the old tasks again, and with such apparent zest and vigour, that many of his friends, deceived perhaps by his sea-bronzed cheeks, began to think that their hopes were to be fulfilled, and that his Australian tour had given him another lease of life. An old colleague, at whose church he preached in April, declared that ' he had ten years' more good work in him.' He was a speaker at the great annual meeting of the Wesleyan Missionary Society, in the Albert Hall, London, and one who heard him at another meeting in Manchester thought that he had rarely spoken so effectively. There were flashes, too, of the old, unconquerable buoyancy of spirit. In one of his very last letters, written from Deganwy to an Australian friend about ten days before his death, he says :—

' We are enjoying a week at sunny Deganwy, where we hoped to have the pleasure of entertaining you and yours. I have just been on the hill at the back of our home. From the little summit I had a fine view of Llandudno, Gloddaeth Woods, the Conway vale, the mountains on the other side of the river, and—right away across the straits—Anglesea, Puffin Island, etc. It is all very lovely. We had set our hearts on showing it all to you. This very morning your letters arrived with the disappointing news that you are not to be with us this year. However, you give us the hope of a visit in the near future. How glad we shall be to renew our fellowship with you all ! . . . Since my return I have been very busy. The Mission had run smoothly and successfully. They reserved any difficulties in changes and extensions for me ; I am now dealing with them under conditions of life and industry that are not helpful. But England is pulling through steadily. I have never seen the people so calm, confident, even hopeful, at such critical times. The clouds are already clearing, and I think we 'll be in brighter days, nationally and internationally, soon.'

In another Deganwy letter, written to one of his sons, a month earlier, it is not easy to say which is the stronger—the impulse to work, or the craving for rest :—

> ' I have been in Manchester (and other places) as busy as possible.  Driven rather too hard, I was fearfully tired on Thursday, and fled here both for my own sake, and in order to arrange mother's return. . . . Everything looks very beautiful this morning and makes one feel tempted to wish a few years' quiet and retired life.  But " the world is in such a condition, and so much depends on action, that everything seems to be crying out loudly to everybody, *Do something* "—Bulwer Lytton ;  but it fits to-day.'

The sad truth is that, after his return from Australia, Collier was never his old self again ;  he had come home only to die.  I do not know that he ever put it in so many words—it was never his way to speak much of himself—but some of those who were near him were conscious of a change in him, as if he had heard a voice say,

> ' It is time to be old,
> To take in sail.'

He tired much more quickly than was his wont ;  he had lost the old quickness in getting the threads of work into his hands ;  the back was no longer equal to the daily burden.  He did his best to conceal the fact. 'However unfit you may feel,' he used to say to his colleagues, 'when you are going into the pulpit or on the platform, never show it. Pull yourself together, and try to appear at your best.' And he acted upon his own counsel. But the time was at hand when the truth could no longer be concealed. He preached for the last time on Whitsunday (May 15). It was a very busy day, though not busier than his Sundays normally were. He conducted the morning service at Union Street Wesleyan Methodist Church, Rochdale. In the afternoon he was motored back for a great open-air service in Heaton Park, Manchester, addressed by the new Bishop (Dr. Temple) and himself. He preached again at Rochdale in the evening, returning home the same night. The next day he was at Cliff College, in Derbyshire, to join in the Whitsuntide anniversary gatherings of his friend, Samuel Chadwick. He complained of a sharp, shooting pain in his side after speaking. On Tuesday, very unwell, he sought refuge in his loved Deganwy, where the letter to his Australian friend quoted above was written. There he remained resting quietly till the following Monday (May 23), when again he returned to Manchester. Obviously unfit though he was, he attended the usual staff meeting on Tuesday morning, and stayed for the mid-day service which followed, at which Dr. F. B. Meyer was the preacher. Immediately afterwards he went for a thorough overhauling at the hands of his doctor. The medical verdict was that he was utterly exhausted, and that complete rest was absolutely imperative. From Tuesday to Friday he was persuaded to remain in bed. Then, despite the remonstrances of his friends, he left his room to attend a Trustees' Meeting at which important business, he thought, rendered his presence necessary. When the business was over he told the meeting the doctor's report. He had made a mistake in plunging at once into the work of the Mission after his long and exhausting tour. ' It is easy to be wise after the event,' he said, ' and I know now that I ought to have rested for a while on the Continent.' The meeting broke up ; Collier shook hands, and turned away to go home. He was never in the Central Hall again.

That night (Friday), after his return, he seemed no worse. Gipsy Smith, who had come to take his Sunday services, was with him, and the two friends chatted together for a long time. The Gipsy tried to persuade him that the time had come when he must resign, and leave the burden of the Mission to others. But Collier would not be persuaded, not yet at least ; there were a few things that he must see through first. The next morning influenza developed, with a high temperature, and the day following, pneumonia and pleurisy. On Tuesday he became unconscious ; the poor, tired heart had no strength for a struggle, and on Thursday (June 2) he was gone. All through the delirium of the last hours, his mind was still busy with the things of the Mission, dictating letters, delivering speeches, treading the old, familiar round. At one time he was concerned about the welfare of some coloured students, whose coming he had been expecting. At another, his mind turned to the Australian cricketers who were that year visiting England. Yet here, too, the Mission was the background of his thoughts ; some of the leading players were going to speak at the Central Hall : ' Before I forget,' he said, ' ring up Cooper and arrange.' Shortly before the end on Thursday, he imagined himself at Bridgewater Hall ; the meeting was just coming to a close ; he announced the familiar Doxology, started the tune, and called on those in the room to join with him.

> ' Even now he sung.
> . . . 'Tis strange that death should sing.'

But his was no ' doleful hymn,' though sung with ' the organ-pipe of frailty.' [1] He greeted the Unseen with a cheer ; he met his Lord with a glad ' *Laus Deo* ' on his lips.

The funeral, which took place on Monday, June 6, at the Southern Cemetery, was one such as Manchester has rarely seen.

> ' The service in the cemetery—I quote from the *Manchester Guardian* of the following day— was of the simplest possible character, but a memorial service was held before it at the Central Hall. The interment was witnessed by a greater press of people than has ever gathered

[1] See Shakespeare's *King John*, Act v. Scene vii.

at the cemetery on any similar occasion. It was an impressive expression of the respect in which Mr. Collier was held in Manchester. In the funeral procession there were a hundred motor-cars bearing friends and representatives of every branch of the religious, political, and social life of the city, and four cars were filled with wreaths alone. The procession was watched by many people along the route from the city; and at the cemetery, on each side of the pathway from the gates to the graveside, men and women were lined up, rank after rank, in a great unbroken sequence. The occasion was marked by an extreme simplicity, in perfect accord with the character of the man in whose honour the vast crowd had assembled.

' The memorial service at the Central Hall was hardly less remarkable than the funeral itself. Two hours before the service began people were taking their places, and at the advertised time every seat in the large hall was filled. It was a representative gathering. On the platform, representing the Corporation, were the Lord Mayor of Manchester and the Chief Constable. Beside the representatives of the Wesleyan community were Canon Peter Green (representing the Dean and Chapter of Manchester Cathedral), the Rev. Dr. Roberts, and Sir Edward Tootal Broadhurst. The Rev. J. Hornabrook conducted the service, and an address was delivered by the Rev. Samuel Chadwick, who had been intimately associated with Mr. Collier from his earliest days.'

To-day the grave is marked by a large cross of Aberdeen granite, placed there by the loving hands of the people to whom he had given his life. On the front of the cross are inscribed these words :—

> ' In Praise to God for the Life of
> The Rev. SAMUEL FRANCIS COLLIER,
> October 3rd, 1855—June 2nd, 1921.
> This Memorial
> To the Founder and First Superintendent
> (1885—1921)
> is erected
> in loving remembrance
> By the Members of the
> Manchester and Salford Wesleyan Mission.'

On the right and on the left of the stone are the names of the two sons, Frank and Sidney, who died in the War.

It has been my privilege to read an immense number of letters and telegrams—some hundreds in all—addressed to Mrs. Collier after her husband's death. They came from men and women of all sorts, in all parts of the world, and taken together they form a very striking and spontaneous tribute to his memory. ' All humanitarian causes,' said the Prime Minister (Mr. Lloyd George), ' are greatly impoverished by Mr. Collier's death.' ' All who care for the religious life of Manchester,' said Bishop Temple, ' are mourning with you.' [1] Mr. J. L. Paton, the High Master of Manchester Grammar School, spoke for a great host of workers for the city's welfare when he said, ' This day the Lord

---

[1] At a service in the Cathedral, the day after Collier's death, the Dean referred to their loss, and at his suggestion the whole congregation stood in silence as a mark of respect and sympathy.

taketh away our head from us.' 'I doubt if any man,' wrote Dr. R. F. Horton, ' ever crowded more service, more achievement, for Christ into sixty-six years. He makes us all feel unprofitable servants.' Others, again, spoke, not so much of the loss to the Church or the community, as of their own sharp, personal bereavement : it was as if something had gone out of their life that could never be replaced. ' Manchester, to me,' said Dr. Campbell Morgan, ' is empty without him. It may be a weak and foolish thing to say, but I say it nevertheless ; I don't feel that I ever want to walk its streets again.' And nowhere, of course, was the sense both of public and private loss so keen as among the members of his own community. ' There is none like him left to us,' wrote one who followed him in the Chair of the Conference. ' Many of us,' said an old colleague, ' have lost our " Master " who taught us most of what we know in Christian work.'

And beside all these was the multitude of those who wrote no letters, who brought no costly wreaths, but whose sorrow was not less real because for the most part it was inarticulate. A week after the funeral a minister took into the Albert Hall a friend who wished to see over the building. A woman was washing the floor in the entrance hall. As she rose from her knees, the minister said to her, ' We have lost a friend.' ' No,' said she simply, correcting him, ' I 've lost a father.' One is reminded of the scene in the upper chamber at Joppa, where Dorcas lay dead. When Peter came, we are told, all the widows stood by him weeping. There is no record of anything they said, but they showed him *on themselves* [1] the coats and garments which Dorcas had made, while she was with them. It was with love like that that thousands followed Collier to his grave, and still cherish his memory in their hearts. When William the Silent died, Motley tells us, the little children cried in the streets. And of all the words that love has spoken in praise of Collier of Manchester none would have been sweeter to his own ear than the unrecorded words spoken in the dwellings of the poor, where for long he will be named softly ' as the household name of one whom God has taken.'

[1] A beautiful little touch (Acts ix. 39) which is missing from both our Authorised and Revised Versions.

# INDEX